DA

# EUROPEAN
# IMPERIALISM
# IN AFRICA

BY

HALFORD LANCASTER HOSKINS

DICKSON PROFESSOR OF HISTORY
TUFTS COLLEGE

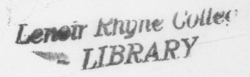

NEW YORK
HENRY HOLT AND COMPANY

19396

April 1943

# PREFACE

The college teacher of general European history is always confronted with the task of finding adequate reading for his classes which is neither too specialized and technical nor too elementary. For many topics, including several of the greatest importance, no such material is at the moment available. Moreover, in too many instances, good reading which undeniably does exist is in the form of a chapter in a larger work and is therefore too expensive for adoption as required reading under normal conditions.

*The Berkshire Studies in European History* have been planned to meet this situation. The topics selected for treatment are those on which there is no easily accessible reading of appropriate length adequate for the needs of a course in general European history. The authors, all experienced teachers, are in nearly every instance actively engaged in the class room and intimately acquainted with its problems. They will avoid a merely elementary presentation of facts, giving instead an interpretive discussion suited to the more mature point of view of college students.

No pretense is made, of course, that these *Studies* are contributions to historical literature in the scholarly sense. Each author, nevertheless, is sufficiently a specialist in the period of which he writes to be familiar with the sources and to have used the latest scholarly contributions to his subject. In order that those who desire to read further on any topic may have some guid-

v

ance short bibliographies of works in western European languages are given, with particular attention to books of recent date.

Each *Study* is designed as a week's reading. The division into three approximately equal chapters, many of them self-contained and each suitable for one day's assignment, should make the series as a whole easily adaptable to the present needs of college classes. The editors have attempted at every point to maintain and emphasize this fundamental flexibility.

Maps and diagrams will occasionally be furnished with the text when specially needed but a good historical atlas, such as that of Shepherd, is presupposed throughout.

R. A. N.
L. B. P.
S. R. P.

# CONTENTS

# EUROPEAN IMPERIALISM IN AFRICA

# CHAPTER I

## EUROPEAN PENETRATION INTO AFRICA

### CHARACTER OF THE AFRICAN CONTINENT

AFRICA has played a strange part in human annals. The seat of one of the earliest civilizations, it has been the last of the continents to assume a prominent place in world affairs. Until late in the fifteenth century, practically all but the Mediterranean lands were unknown to Europe, and only during the last half century has this ceased to be the "dark continent." Africa's long isolation from world affairs has not been due to size, for it is the second largest of the earth's land masses, having an area of 11,608,000 square miles. Nor can it be ascribed to location, for its position on the globe, with reference to the Equator, the oceans, and other large land masses, is distinctly strategic. Yet from early medieval until very recent times the continent as a whole has loomed up as a huge barrier to the natural activities of European peoples.

The anomaly is explained by the fact that Africa is peculiarly difficult of approach. It has fewer miles of seacoast than Europe, which boasts less than a third the area of Africa. Regularity of coast line entails a paucity of points of human access, such as sheltered bays, harbors and islands, and this serious lack has been a great factor in Africa's tardy development. But even from the coast lands themselves the interior of the continent is not easily reached. Ranges of rugged hills and mountains, at irregular distances from, but roughly parallel to, the coast on every side, form considerable barriers. African rivers, too, are generally disappointing. The few streams whose volume is adequate for purposes of navigation almost invariably reach the sea through their deltas in numerous small tortuous streams, choked with mud and sand banks, wholly incapable of accommodating vessels of any considerable size. Farther up in their courses they break through the continental mountain ranges in such series of rapids and cascades as effectually to bar the way to the ready passage of boats into their fertile drainage basins. The coastal plains themselves have not usually been of a character to attract peoples from other lands and climates. Combinations of low elevation and proximity to the Equator, or lack of rainfall and sterility of soil, to which may be added the myriad diseases of marsh and jungle in the tropics, have repeatedly foiled the most persistent efforts of white men to establish footholds in Africa.

It should be noted at this point, however, that few generalizations can be used in speaking of the African continent. Aside from a remarkably uniform, even monotonous, continental outline, Africa is far from being a unit in any sense. Ranges of mountains, degrees of elevation, extreme variations in climate and rainfall, fundamental variations among aboriginal races, and the relative proximity of other continental areas, separate Africa into a number of fairly well defined and often sharply contrasting regions.

Almost the whole interior of the continent consists

of a vast tableland much broken up by mountains and deep river valleys. While the high elevations of the continental plateau with its mountainous fringes produce a tolerable climate even under the Equator, they also militate against an adequate and equable distribution of rainfall. Much of the interior of the continent consequently is more or less arid. The Sahara Desert, which forms a broad belt almost entirely across the widest part of the continent, and the Kalahari Desert in the south, represent extreme phases of a tendency marked in nearly all parts of the interior. The greater part of the Congo basin, however, lying at a lower elevation, presents every kind of contrast with other natural divisions of the continent.

A further illustration of the absence of cohesion in the structure of Africa is found in that portion of the continent which faces Europe across the 'Mediterranean. Separated from more southern regions by the Atlas Mountains and the great Sahara Desert and sloping toward an inland sea, it is not strange that this continental fringe has had a history very largely dissociated from that of the rest of the land-mass. This same tendency is even more conspicuously marked in the case of Egypt, which, largely isolated by the Libyan Desert and the uplands forming the northern boundary of the Sudan, where the navigation of the Nile ceases, belongs both geographically and historically perhaps more to the Near East than to Africa.

At the same time, the obstacles to outside penetration which have been enumerated should not obscure the fact that Africa has much to offer to people coming from any other quarter of the globe. Considerable portions of the continent are well adapted for agriculture, other sections for the harvesting of the many valuable products of the tropics, while immense areas are naturally adapted to the grazing industry. To these natural advantages should be added the mineral and other resources with which many of the habitable regions are generously endowed.

These considerations may serve to emphasize the fact that Africa, instead of constituting a natural unit as far as human needs and interests are concerned, comprises a group of regions facing in all directions away from the centre of the continent. A survey of the geographical bearings of Africa will largely assist a clear understanding of the reason for the long obscurity of the continent as a whole and an appreciation of the setting for a period of fierce international rivalry, once physical and bacterial obstructions had been partially surmounted by the technological and hygienic progress of European peoples.

### EARLY CONTACTS WITH EUROPE

Africa has been the home of many and diverse races since very early times. Whence and when these came has been a matter of considerable speculation. Certainly many of them—Asiatic Negroes, Caucasian types, Polynesians and Malays, Hamites and Semites —are not indigenous to Africa. Within historic times various alien peoples whose movements can be traced have migrated to Africa. Across the land bridge into Egypt came successive waves of Asiatics: ancient peoples from Asia Minor, Syria and Mesopotamia; fanatical Mohammedans from Arabia after 640 A.D.;

plundering Turks in 1517 and afterward; to mention but a few. Among the migrants from Europe were, consecutively, Greeks and Romans, barbarous Vandals and expropriated Moors, and, in later times, Italians, French and Spanish, with sprinklings of more northern peoples. These established themselves in the lands bordering the Mediterranean Sea and were almost as ignorant of the remainder of Africa as were their more northern contemporaries.

Below the Mediterranean fringe during these centuries Africa was inhabited and fought over by numerous "native" peoples of widely varied origins, ranging all the way from depraved Bushmen and lowly Hottentots to the relatively advanced Bantu and Bushongo peoples. This racial and cultural diversity, in conjunction with the physical features of Africa, proved to be a prolific source of difficult problems to Europeans intent on opening up and exploiting the continent in the nineteenth century.

During much of the historic period, European contacts with Africa were slight or non-existent. Accounts of early voyages of circumnavigation of Africa receive little credence. The lines extending across the Mediterranean in the days of antiquity were broken with the decline of the Roman Empire. The Crusades, beginning at the close of the eleventh century, somewhat increased European knowledge of the Mediterranean lands. Indirectly they contributed much to the eventual opening up of the whole continent by giving rise to large demands for oriental goods and by promoting the idea that a sea route around Africa would circumvent the Mohammedan barrier in Egypt and

Syria and provide a practicable route to the sources of those goods.

Yet the discovery of the all-sea route and the growth of interest in Africa were due less to the limitations of the old Mohammedan-controlled routes than to new impulses inherent in the rapid development of western Europe. The emergence of the Atlantic seaboard nation-states in the fifteenth century, the lessening of internecine warfare, and the growth of populations ushered in a remarkable period of discovery, exploration and trade, which laid the foundations for later political expansion.

In the business of pushing back the horizon, Portugal was peculiarly fitted to take the lead because of strategic position, political solidarity, strength of motives, and dynastic leadership. The first important step in the disclosing of Africa was taken when the Portuguese, having expelled the Moslems from Portugal, followed them to the coast of Morocco, and there, across the straits from Gibraltar, in 1415, seized the key position of Ceuta. With this infidel stronghold as a base, Portuguese mariners crept down the West Coast of Africa in search of some natural passage to the East. For a long while the only tangible accomplishment was the rediscovery of the Madeira and Azores island groups. As the work of exploration progressed, the discovery of sources of gold dust, ivory, and Negro slaves gave economic impulse to the initial motives of science and religion. The death of Prince Henry the Navigator in 1460 interrupted but did not stop the exploring process, which found its logical culmination in Vasco da Gama's justly celebrated voyage to India in 1497.

These and subsequent activities of the Portuguese gave promise of early penetration into the interior of Africa. Yet nearly four centuries remained before this promise was fulfilled. The exploits which disclosed the outlines and something of the resources of the great continent also opened up a practicable all-water route to India, Persia, and the Moluccas, and these regions, rather than Africa, early proved to be the lands of commercial reward. Da Gama's first voyage to India, although purely a pioneering venture and handicapped by long delays, shipwrecks and great expense, still returned more than sixty times its cost in profits. Extensive trade with Africa therefore awaited the further growth of European commercial demands.

### POSTS AND FACTORIES OF THE EARLY MODERN ERA

The Portuguese, nevertheless, left some impress on the continent of Africa. As a part of their policy of controlling the eastern seas and the route thereto, they established garrisons at nearly all the strategic points along the entire African coast from Ceuta to Cape Guardafui. Only at one point was their plan notably at fault: the southern tip of the continent, almost the only natural door to the vast interior, was left entirely unoccupied to serve as a vantage point for later European rivals.

Africa was generally regarded as a kind of Portuguese preserve during most of the fifteenth and sixteenth centuries, for Portuguese prestige was high in Europe and it was not widely understood that their hold was largely superficial and struck deeply at only a few points. Only in Mozambique and Angola, which still remain as monuments to the enterprise of their missions and slaving stations, did the Portuguese language partially take root. But the nation which had accomplished wonders in the days of Da Gama, Almeida and Albuquerque quickly burned itself out. Numerous causes of internal decay were capped by forcible annexation to Spain in 1580. In the ensuing attacks from more northern nations, dominion in Africa melted rapidly away.

Among the first to invade the Portuguese African monopoly were the English. Soon after the middle of the sixteenth century semi-piratical mariner-merchants began venturing to the Guinea Coast for gold or slaves. The destruction of the Great Armada in 1588 removed much of the apprehension of Hispanic sea power previously felt by England's virgin Queen, who no longer hesitated to charter monopolistic concerns for the African trade. So while the French busied themselves in Senegambia and the Dutch acquired footholds in Gorée, Arguin, and at the Cape of Good Hope, the English built numerous forts along the Guinea Coast and developed some trade on the Niger River.

The seventeenth century saw considerable competition along the West Coast. As North American and West Indian colonies sprang up, the African slave trade became increasingly profitable. By 1700 the English Royal African Company had perhaps twenty or more fortified factories between the Gambia and Congo Rivers, but as four or five other nations were actively operating in the same region, rivalry was bitter and posts frequently changed hands. The English trade fell off after 1750, partly because of the greater attractions in the East Indies and elsewhere, partly because of the growth of anti-slavery sentiment in England. This, however, did not prevent the English from supplanting most of their rivals in Africa during the series of wars which ended in 1815.

The Dutch, while sharing in the trade of the Guinea Coast, had meanwhile established themselves at other points as their Eastern interests developed. About the middle of the seventeenth century their East India Company occupied Table Bay, from which point of vantage the whole Cape Peninsula was gradually settled. But this, although a true colony, which other African posts were not, failed to prosper because of the short-sighted policy of the Dutch Company in excluding free settlers and in exploiting its resident servants. These, therefore, pushed into the interior, enslaving or ousting the natives and generating a numerous half-caste population to perplex the administrations of later times.

The French also had arrived early on the scene and had established themselves between the Senegal and Gambia Rivers. A period of conflict ensued with the Dutch, Danes and English. The French managed to hold on, however, and they had penetrated some distance into the interior before they were dispossessed by the British during the wars of the late eighteenth century. The restoration of the stations on the Senegal in 1817 made possible the development of a great West African empire during the nineteenth century.

French traders, however, had not confined themselves to the West Coast during the early period; they partially replaced the Dutch in Madagascar and in the Indian Ocean. This contributed largely to the plots, first of the Bourbon monarchy and later of the Directory, to acquire Egypt in order to establish an overland route to India, but Bonaparte's expedition of 1798 failed, and conditions were never again so favorable for the French.

At one time or another still other European nations had sampled the African trade. The Danes appeared on the Gold Coast in the seventeenth century and established slaving stations which operated for a century and a half. The Brandenburgers after 1683 made a brief attempt to capture some of the African trade. Even the Spanish retained a few posts not restored to Portugal in 1640. But while all of the nations except the Belgians, which were eventually to partition the continent, were on the ground by the beginning of the eighteenth century, their competition was confined to the realm of trade in such articles as were ready at hand. Territorial rivalry on a large scale had not yet been dreamed of. Politically, Europe was ready for great accomplishments after the Congress of Vienna and bases for action had long since been planted on African coasts, but the changes which were to bring practically the entire African continent into the European political and economic sphere still awaited the transforming power of the Industrial Revolution.

BRITISH INTERESTS IN SOUTH AFRICA

That portion of the African continent which became the scene of European colonization on the largest scale was the portion most neglected during the early modern era. The southern extremity of the continent had been known since the voyage of Bartholomew Diaz in 1486. During the early years of the sixteenth century Portuguese vessels occasionally put in at Table Bay for fresh water and other supplies. But a dangerous coast and the hostile attitude of the natives gained for the region an unsavory reputation and caused it long to be avoided.

Among the successors of the Portuguese, the English displayed an early but ephemeral interest in the Cape. The Dutch, however, found it both convenient and strategic as a way station to their eastern possessions, and in 1652 their East India Company located about a hundred of its servants at Table Bay. From this small beginning sprang a true colony which, by the close of the eighteenth century, numbered some fifteen thousand settlers.

The European wars which marked the advent of the nineteenth century brought an end to Dutch control of the colony. Having been taken by British naval forces in 1795 and again in 1806, the colony, on payment of an indemnity to the Dutch, was allotted in the settlement of 1815 to that Power which then had greatest need of a supply depot on the all-sea route to India.

But the new acquisition was unexpectedly endowed with difficulties. From the first the English military administration had to deal with serious complications, most of which sprang from unsatisfactory relations between whites and natives.  Of the latter, three distinct races contributed to the colony's problems: the Bushmen, a weak, degraded stock; the Hottentots, stronger than the Bushmen; and the Bantus or Kaffirs, a virile, aggressive, intelligent race of blacks.  The Boers, white farmers of Dutch and French Huguenot origin, had easily enslaved or driven out the Bushmen and Hottentots, but their first clashes with the southward-moving Bantus left the honors about even.

This unpromising situation was considerably aggravated by the early arrival in South Africa of English missionaries.  From the outset they sympathized with the native as against the Boer and their influence among the blacks, on the one hand, and their reports to British authorities of Boer cruelty and injustice, on the other, quickly created a situation in which the Boer was denied an impartial hearing.  He was naturally highly indignant at English championship of the savages, whom he had come to regard at the worst as a sort of vermin and at the best as divinely ordained to subserve the white man's needs.

Biased reports from South Africa contributed materially to the passage in 1833 of a Parliamentary Act abolishing slavery throughout British dominions.  This not only removed the principal source of labor supply in South Africa but provided compensation on the most inadequate basis, leaving the Boer with the suspicion that he was marked for ruin.  Suspicion ripened into conviction when, after the Boers had repulsed some murderous Kaffir attacks in 1834, the British

Colonial Office compelled restitution of all Kaffir property seized.

The Boer cup of grievance was full. It began with racial and language prejudice against the English. It was aggravated by differences and contrasts in religious and moral codes, culture, political theory and views on slavery. Consequently, in 1835 and 1836 small groups of Voortrekkers, as the first migrants were called, crossed the Orange River to escape from British sovereignty. During the next four years, some ten thousand others followed their example, and, displacing the natives along the lines of march, founded small, loosely constructed republics in the wilderness.

Even here the long arm of Britain followed. Troubles with the Zulus in Natal in 1838 and a due regard for the value of seacoast led the British Government in 1843 to assume control over the entire region south of Portuguese East Africa. Then no sooner had many of the Boers withdrawn from Natal to the region between the Orange and Vaal Rivers than it was annexed (1848) as the Orange River Sovereignty. Partial emancipation was obtained, however, in the unclaimed wilderness north of the Vaal River, where, by the Sand River Convention in 1852, the Boers received the right of governing themselves under stipulated conditions. This served as a precedent for a similar convention with the Orange Free State in 1854, where the expense and difficulty of a British administration were not counterbalanced by the meagre advantages.

It can scarcely be said that even after surmounting such difficulties the future of the Boer republics appeared auspicious. They were entirely isolated from the outside world and almost surrounded by large groups of dispossessed and warlike natives. They were pledged to avoid any form of exploitation of these wards of the British Government. Boundaries, too, were ill defined. Even so, the next two decades were years of substantial, if not peaceful, development. These were also years of growth in the Cape Colony. Immigration from the British Isles considerably increased and full responsible government was attained in 1872. Natal, too, in 1856 embarked on its own career as a crown colony.

Such developments and the growth of imperialistic sentiment at home were important factors in the opening of a new period of friction with the Boers. This was introduced by the creation of new British protectorates in Basutoland and Griqualand between 1866 and 1871, which encroached on both flanks of the Orange River Boers, inhibiting normal expansion. Zulu threats in 1876 next provided the home Government, then in the hands of Disraeli and the colonial-minded Conservatives, with the argument that territorial consolidation in South Africa was the only practicable means of solving native questions and protecting the whites. Accordingly, after the most cursory investigation, the British flag was raised at Pretoria in April 1, 1877, and the Transvaal was declared annexed.

As a guarantee of peace, this act was ill judged. Some of the Boers rose in arms; nearly all were furious at what they considered British perfidy, and none more so than Oom Paul Kruger, future President of the

Transvaal and author of the war for independence. Even the impending Zulu war was not averted, and a sanguinary and nearly disastrous campaign was necessary before Zululand could be made into a British protectorate. From the annexation of the Transvaal in 1877 the sequence of events leading to the Boer War is a well-blazed trail. It is a record of errors and misunderstanding founded on thousands of miles of distance between administrative authority and scene of action, and on fundamental differences between the active, persistent British merchant, mine operator or land speculator of the nineteenth century and the stolid, transplanted and isolated Dutch farmer of the seventeenth century. Rash moves and ill-timed vacillation presently carried the issues beyond the possibility of compromise.

### THE FRENCH CONQUEST OF ALGERIA

The acquisition by the British of a convenient position at the southern tip of Africa at the beginning of the nineteenth century was soon counterbalanced by a French establishment on the northern edge of the continent. France had recovered slowly from the economic and spiritual depression induced by the total loss of her first colonial empire. Although there were relatively few obstacles to the resumption of French colonial enterprise after the Congress of Vienna, the French Government was apparently impressed with the futility of investing work and treasure in regions which might be difficult to protect. However, the recovery of the old French sphere at the mouth of the Senegal and a few scattered islands contributed to a gradual revival of interest in colonial matters as France once more assumed her normal place among the powers. The brief reign of Charles X marks the opening of a new period of French expansion overseas.

France had maintained commercial relations with the Mohammedan states of North Africa for decades. In order to insure this trade against Barbary pirate raids, it had long been customary to pay annual subsidies to the Moslem chiefs. These payments had been suspended during the Napoleonic Wars, however, and piratical activity had been resumed in the Mediterranean. After the Congress of Vienna, various Christian Powers sent punitive expeditions into North African waters, exacting promises of good behavior from the Barbary rulers which were as often violated.

It was the able and unscrupulous Polignac, minister and confidant of Charles X, who saw in the situation in North Africa a potential panacea for political unrest in France and a means for the full recovery of French prestige abroad. Noting the preoccupation of the Powers with the Greek question, he evolved a scheme whereby France might use the interested but equally astute Pasha of Egypt, Mehemet Ali, as a cat's-paw in securing to France the guardianship of the Mediterranean by intervention in the Barbary states. A timely pretext for forceful action in the regency of Algiers was supplied in 1827, when the Dey on a public occasion deliberately and grievously insulted the French Consul. By way of retribution, the Algerian coast was immediately blockaded and plans were prepared by which Mehemet Ali would assume the responsibility for carrying out in Algeria "a simple police operation, with the moral and financial support of a friendly government."

A few decades earlier such plans probably would have received little criticism. The world had been shrinking rapidly since the close of the eighteenth century, however, and now a military and naval operation on the southern shores of the Mediterranean could not be disguised as an international missionary enterprise and so escape unchallenged. Great Britain in particular, alarmed for the safety of her newly projected highway to India and the East, refused to sanction any move which might make the Mediterranean a "French lake." The Turkish Sultan refused even nominal support to the imperialistic designs of his over-ambitious Egyptian vassal, who had already failed to come to terms with France. Even at home Polignac found an unexpected chorus of opposition to his "Grand Dessein," and carried on only against ever-increasing odds. For many months he attempted to disarm criticism aimed at the extensive military and naval preparations being made in French Mediterranean ports by insisting on French disinterestedness in African territory. But strenuous British objections to an Algerian expedition were waived only when the French Government issued a formal statement denying all imperialistic intentions and promising to make no change in the political status of Algeria without the consent of the leading European Powers.

The expedition which in May, 1830, did sail to reduce the Algerian strongholds fully justified British fears by going far beyond its advertised objectives.

Before the end of July, 1830, all of the principal Algerian ports were in French hands, thirty thousand French soldiers were encamped on Algerian soil, and reinforcements were pouring in. Without any reference to the political rights of the Ottoman Empire or the sentiments of other European states, a convention was imposed on the Dey which in substance made Algeria a French protectorate. Yet up to the very hour of the July Revolution, which ended the Bourbon monarchy and enthroned the house of Orleans in France, assurances of an early evacuation of Algeria were being given to the watching Powers.

The new French King, Louis Philippe, for the most part unembarrassed by the formal pledges of his predecessor, treated the conquest of Algeria as an accomplished fact. Far from withdrawing from the regency, his government took advantage of the wave of revolution which swept over Europe and of a crisis in the Near East to embark on a program of consolidation, pacification and Gallicization in Algeria which laid the basis for a new colonial empire. The capture of Algerian ports provided footholds, but by no means implied the subjugation of the scattered tribes of the hinterland, where even the Dey's authority had never been more than nominal. Large reinforcements, improved generalship, and a determination to complete the conquest carried French arms rapidly forward after 1840, however, and within a score of years the pacification and reorganization of the new colony had been accomplished.

The occupation of Algeria was the first tangible step in the European recovery of North Africa, but there was little in the early history of French dominion to inspire further appropriation of African territory by European Powers. The conquest alone had involved the loss of about one hundred and fifty thousand lives and the expenditure of upwards of six hundred million dollars. Moreover, for many years Algeria gave little promise of becoming more than a source of trouble and expense. But French disasters during the Franco-German War of 1870-1 heralded the dawn of a brighter day in Algeria, for here the French sought compensation for the loss of Alsace-Lorraine and found solace for war ills in carrying out a really enlightened program. This rested on the then novel idea of enlisting the co-operation of the native population. By incorporating the colony as an integral part of France and investing enormous sums in railways, land improvements and public utilities, this has largely been achieved. Algeria stands today as one of the most successful, if not the most profitable, of modern colonial enterprises.

## EUROPEAN INTERESTS IN EGYPT

For several centuries prior to the nineteenth European contacts with Egypt had been slight. The overlordship of the Sultan of Turkey was manifested by a pasha in Cairo, but real control of Egypt resided in a self-perpetuating body of twenty-four Mameluke Beys, whose incessant intrigues kept the country in a state bordering on chaos. But the valley of the Nile was potentially too rich commercially and too strategically located to continue being neglected by the rising Powers in Western Europe. France had cherished certain shadowy claims in the Levant since the days of the crusading Louis IX, and from the time of Louis XIV, with the decline of the Ottoman Empire, had marked Egypt for her own. During the latter half of the eighteenth century, the English East India Company developed a profitable trade in the Red Sea and, when political conditions permitted, maintained a precarious route through Egypt for Indian despatches. As the eastern trade also manifested a certain tendency to return to this natural highway from which the Turks had largely driven it, Great Britain began to regard the country with a jealous eye. On the outcome of Anglo-French contests rested the future of Egypt.

After several years of sparring, the Egyptian question came to the fore early in the career of Napoleon Bonaparte. "In order really to destroy England," he said in 1797, "it will be necessary to seize Egypt." His powerful expedition of the following year did succeed temporarily in setting up a French régime, but the destruction of his fleet at Aboukir, an abortive campaign in Syria, and Anglo-Turkish and Anglo-Indian invasions of Egypt brought an end to his project in 1801. Upon the withdrawal of British troops two years later, the country again relapsed into a species of anarchy.

Out of this welter rose the striking figure of Mehemet Ali. Beginning his career as a subordinate officer in a Turkish Albanian levy, he rose within a few years by treachery and slaughter to be Turkish Pasha and all but independent sovereign of Egypt. His establishment of domestic tranquillity, his ambitions, his appreciation of western institutions and his shrewd estimate of European interests quickly placed Egypt in a conspicuous position and gave rise to more than one grave crisis in Anglo-French relations.

The factors in what may be called the Egyptian Question long remained constant. The goal of Mehemet Ali was the establishment of an independent dynasty in Egypt with such additional territories as he might find means to acquire. In this the French were ever willing to assist for the double purpose of making Egypt a dependent satellite and of competing successfully with Great Britain for leadership in the Levant. Aside from the conviction that the safety of Europe rested on the integrity of the Ottoman Empire, Great Britain after 1825 became more and more interested in Egypt as an essential position on the Red Sea route to India, which for mails, despatches and passengers rapidly supplanted that by way of the Cape of Good Hope.

The political condition of Egypt was thus a vital matter to British eastern interests. Another Power under these circumstances might have found it advisable to abandon the principle of the integrity of Turkey and to seize Egypt as its share in the resulting partition. At this period, however, Great Britain was apprehensive of the complications which might arise from the control of Egypt and preferred to protect national enterprise in the Levant through the subservient Turkish Government. This attitude was strengthened both by British belief in the Pasha's French sympathies and by the care taken by him, even during the Anglo-Egyptian hostilities in 1840, to permit nothing to interfere with the regular use of the overland route through Egypt, the importance of which he clearly comprehended.

Once the route through Egypt was established, the question of its improvement became prominent. A ship canal, either from the Nile to the Red Sea or across the Isthmus of Suez, had long been considered impracticable. New surveys made late in the administration of Mehemet Ali, indicating the engineering feasibility of a sea level canal, interested the French, but evoked the strongest expressions of condemnation from the British Prime Minister, Lord Palmerston, Sir Stratford Canning, Ambassador to the Porte, and others high in British official circles. Such a waterway, in their estimation, would create a "second Bosphorus," severing Africa from Asia and giving rise to serious international problems. It therefore became their self-imposed task to make a ship canal appear the more impracticable as it became the more possible from financial and technical points of view.

An Egyptian railway was held to be a different matter. An iron band from Alexandria to Suez would not alter the geographical status of Egypt and hence was to be desired. Such a line was commenced under English auspices soon after the accession of Abbas in 1849. But his death six years later, by elevating the Francophile Said, brought the Suez Canal idea again to the fore. That this became a leading issue in European diplomacy during the next fifteen years was due chiefly to the acumen and enterprise of Ferdinand de Lesseps, who, late in 1854, secured from the Pasha a preliminary concession for the construction of an isthmian waterway. He was soon to find that, although an Egyptian railway might be constructed on the authority of the Pasha alone, a ship canal required the assent of the Turkish Government. Inasmuch as British influence was strongly entrenched at Constantinople, it appeared doubtful for a number of years whether Turkish approval might ever be secured.

Meanwhile, the completion of the railway to Suez in 1858 still left an obvious need for a commercial waterway. In the following year, therefore, and on the sole authority of the Pasha, a Suez Canal Company was formed in Paris and work, frequently interrupted by British machinations, was begun on the waterway. It was not until 1866 that pressure from France and other European countries obtained from the Porte a definite *firman* making possible the completion of the canal in 1869 despite every kind of obstruction.

Yet the Suez Canal was essentially British from the first. Seventy-five per cent of the vessels paying canal tolls during the first year flew the British flag. Contests arising over the methods of the Company generally resulted in British victories. The purchase by the British Government in 1875 of a large block of Canal shares from the impecunious Khedive, Ismail, while leaving uncertain the precise status of the Government as a stockholder, left no doubt as to the real source of control of the waterway. But the truth of the warning issued by English Liberals, that between remaining altogether aloof from responsibilities in Egypt and acquiring full political control there was no middle ground, still remained to be demonstrated. The Egyptian Railway might have sufficed for purposes of communication, but the Canal quickly became the most vital artery in the English commercial system. Its protection eventually required more than a stockholder's interest in the operating company.

## THE OCCUPATION OF EGYPT

A period of tenseness in European affairs in 1878 coincided with the development of a crisis in Egypt, where the Khedive at last was wholly unable to keep pace with his financial obligations. In consequence, Ismail was practically compelled to fill the more important Egyptian administrative posts with British and French experts, who, without other authority or assistance, were charged with bringing order out of confusion. But lacking the co-operation of the Khedive, constructive work was wholly out of the question, and in April, 1879, the plan fell through. Ismail's extravagances thereupon resumed their sway.

Out of this situation came one of the first intimations of a change in the traditional German policy of non-participation in extra-European politics. While Great Britain and France debated what course next to pursue, Prince Bismarck demanded of the Porte the immediate deposition of Ismail, significantly conveying the idea of intervention in Egypt as an alternative. Britain and France, suddenly galvanized into action, also requested a change in administration and Ismail was shortly afterward apprised of his removal in favor of his son, Tewfik.

These events ushered in the so-called Dual Control —an Anglo-French financial administration acting theoretically for the Powers. The plan of making the Khedive financially a European ward, while leaving him otherwise his usual powers, gave some promise of success until it was interrupted by a mild revolt of lately demobilized Egyptian troops, headed by an ignorant peasant-officer, Ahmed Arabi. The first vague objectives of this movement were soon cleverly turned by the Khedive into an anti-European and crudely national uprising early in 1882.

A situation so threatening could not fail to create much apprehension in Europe. An ill-advised Anglo-French note promising assistance to the Khedive only played into Arabi's hand and aggravated an already dangerous situation. Attempts to secure united action by the Powers failed and only injured the susceptibilities of the Porte. Meanwhile, the prompt sending of an Anglo-French naval expedition to Egyptian waters to exert a moral influence had the effect of precipitating a fanatical outburst of racial hatred in Alexandria, where, on June 11, a number of Europeans were killed and much property was destroyed. In view of the emergency, Admiral Seymour, in charge of the joint expedition, was vested with certain discretionary powers by his Government.

As the situation in Alexandria showed no signs of improvement, he determined to take full advantage of these, and so advised his French colleagues. In Paris, however, the new Freycinet Ministry, apprehensive of German ill will and mindful of the difficulties and dangers which attended their intervention in Tunis,[1] was unwilling to join in the proposed attack

---

[1] See p. 49.

on Alexandria. The French fleet consequently withdrew from the scene and left the British to solve the problem in their own way unhampered and unassisted. Although without imperialistic motives, the British Liberals could not but recognize a really unique opportunity for establishing a paramount interest in the essential Egyptian link in the route to India, for as the news from Egypt grew constantly more gloomy, the Powers, singly or in groups, tacitly disclaimed any responsibility for the outcome. British determination at last to cast aside her traditional policy of nonintervention in Egypt was thundered unmistakably from the guns of Admiral Seymour's fleet as Alexandria was bombarded on July 11. Armed intervention ended dual control.

Having taken the plow alone, the British Government did not look back. Military preparations were made for a complete restoration of order. The Suez Canal was seized, regardless of the protests of the French officials of the Suez Canal Company, a British army was landed at Ismailia, and on September 13 Arabi's motley forces were completely crushed at Tel-el-Kebir without need of the military unit which came out from India to take part in the imperial adventure. With Great Britain thus pledged to order in Egypt, a new definition of policy was needed.

Early in 1883 Gladstone, the "Little Englander," declared it to be the intention of his Government to reseat the Khedive, reconstitute the country, and then to withdraw completely, leaving the future of Egypt in the hands of its own people. Effective Turkish control, of course, was out of the question. While there is no need to question the sincerity of this plan, its realization was made extremely unlikely because of the time element involved. In both strategic and commercial respects the Suez Canal yearly became more important to British interests, and no hazards to its security could be contemplated. Casual interest in the Sudan as the source of the life-giving Nile presently became a recognized responsibility. Both Egypt and the Sudan became enmeshed in the English economic system to a degree that acted powerfully on the national policy with regard to these countries. The very fact of possession eventually produced its own justification and came to be accepted by the other Powers much as had French control in Algeria. With the passage of time, therefore, British withdrawal from Egypt became more and more hypothetical. France found compensation in Tunis and Morocco. The German Empire reached into East, West, and Southwest Africa. Russia was satisfied in Central and Eastern Asia. Austria was preoccupied in the Balkans. Long before the opening of the World War, the retention of Egypt by Great Britain was everywhere taken for granted.

The British régime, while outwardly temporary and informal, was none the less effective. As before, tribute was paid to the Sultan, the Khedive selected his own ministers, and foreign nations enjoyed extensive privileges under the Turkish Capitulations, a group of special treaties the first of which was concluded in 1454. In reality, however, authority resided in the British High Commissioner, whose acts were guided, in turn, by instructions from the British

Foreign Office. Under a series of remarkable administrators, the most notable of whom was Sir Evelyn Baring, later Lord Cromer, who was *de facto* ruler of Egypt for nearly a quarter of a century, the condition of the country rapidly improved. Irrigation was widely extended, roads were built, the culture of tobacco and cotton was greatly improved, and the number of peasant landowners was largely increased as population grew.

Until the opening of the World War, the safety of the Suez Canal was sufficiently guaranteed by a series of international conventions neutralizing that artery. The exigencies of war, however, raised new problems both with regard to the protection of the canal and the status of Great Britain in Egypt. Upon the adhesion of Turkey to the cause of the Central Powers, the British occupation was replaced, in December, 1914, by a formal protectorate.

For the first time military defences were then begun along the line of the canal, barely in time to repulse strong attacks of Turkish forces in 1914 and 1915, and large British forces were detained in Egypt throughout the remainder of the conflict to insure the safety of this vital line of communication.

The relative tranquillity of Egypt during the War gave little hint of problems which were to follow closely after. Post-war psychology and the new doctrine of the rights of the lesser nations combined to breed in Egypt something more akin to national sentiment than ever had been achieved previously. Widespread unrest and sundry disorders led to the investigations of the notable Milner Commission in 1919. Out of this came the recognition of Egypt as a nation in the Milner-Zaghlul Agreement of 1920 and the abandonment of the protectorate a year later. On March 16, 1922, Sultan Ahmed Fuad Pasha became King of Egypt.

This, however, did not signify the withdrawal of Great Britain from Egypt. The essential elements of control were merely perpetuated in the form of conventions and engagements, in which the most essential British interests have been safeguarded and certain rights of intervention recognized. Great Britain has retained the right of taking any measures which may seem necessary for the protection of imperial communications. This right, having been translated into army barracks, aerodromes, naval yards and diplomatic establishments, has been viewed by Egyptian nationalists quite properly as in a measure qualifying their independence. This remains the principal source of friction, though diplomatic negotiations continue on the basis of the limitation of British treaty rights in Egypt and the recognition of Egyptian interests in the Sudan.

# CHAPTER II

## THE PARTITION OF THE CONTINENT

PRIOR to 1870 no European Power had contemplated an extension of its territorial holdings in Africa such as would suggest the near approach of an era of unbridled annexations and diplomatic crises. With few exceptions the African possessions of Europe were inconsiderable both in extent and in value. They were confined for the most part to seaports and fortified trading stations together with bits of adjacent territory acquired at one time or another as adjuncts of trade and never as bases for colonial expansion. Even the adjacent spheres of influence were not extensive. With the termination of the European slave trade many of the factories had been all but abandoned, and few were thriving centres of legitimate trade. The two principal scenes of enterprise lay at opposite ends of the continent in French Algeria and British South Africa, where actual colonization had taken place but with no very tangible objectives in view. Egypt was soon to pass under the joint control of Great Britain and France, but only as a means of protecting the recently completed canal artery and European financial investments and without any definite view to annexation on the part of either of the tutelary Powers.

Elsewhere, France possessed the lower Senegal River, a small post southeast of Cape Verde at Mellicouri, and a bit of the Ivory Coast. Slight contacts were maintained with the north coast of Madagascar. A portion of the Gabun River was claimed, and a single post, Obock, had been acquired on the East Coast at the head of the Gulf of Aden. The British, besides their Cape territories, held trading posts at Bathurst and on the Oil Rivers at the mouths of the Niger. The Portuguese claimed extensive but indefinite tracts on the West Coast, extending from the mouth of the Congo perhaps to the Nourse River, and likewise the whole of Mozambique on the East Coast, but their actual settlements and trading posts were few and scattered. They also held a small foothold on the Guinea Coast, and the islands of Principe and São Thomé in the adjacent Gulf—mere remnants of their former greatness. The Spanish asserted a rather vague claim to a portion of the Northwest Coast known as the Rio de Oro and held a small area on the Rio Muni. Aside from these possessions, many of which were more nominal than real, there were essentially no European interests in Africa. The Danes had withdrawn after the sale of their former possessions in 1850 and the Dutch had been completely eliminated in 1872. The day of the Belgians, Germans, and Italians had not yet dawned.

Much of the interior of Africa, however, had ceased to be veiled in darkness. Since the early part of the century, the human barriers which had long obstructed the light had been breaking down. Dealers in Negro slaves no longer maintained their jealous hold along the West Coast; hostile natives no longer dominated South Africa; and Mohammedan fanaticism was not proof against European penetration in the North. Through breaches made at these points European explorers and missionaries had boldly pushed their way, and by 1870 had already solved many mysteries and disclosed to an interested world some of the potentialities of the continent.

Even before the close of the Napoleonic Wars the first of a long series of attacks had been made on the interior of "darkest Africa," of which little more than the bare outlines had previously been known. Between 1769 and 1773 a Scotchman, James Bruce, found the source of the Blue Nile and drew some attention to Abyssinia. Egypt, only roughly known before, became gradually more familiar after 1770 as English and French trading vessels came with greater frequency from India to Cosseir and Suez and increasing numbers of Europeans passed through the country on official missions. Surveys and descriptions by the savants of Bonaparte's expedition of 1798 brought Egypt really within the European horizon.

Only a short time before, in 1795, Mungo Park had first reached the Niger River from the British post on the Gambia. In 1805 he returned to complete the survey but perished at the hands of the natives. In 1818-1819 Tripoli and Fezzan were explored by the Englishmen Ritchie and Lyon. Seven years later Major Alexander Laing reached the forbidden city of Timbuktu, but perished during the exploit, and it remained for the Frenchman, René Caillié, to complete the survey of the upper Niger. At the same time, in 1823, a strong expedition, of which Commander Hugh Clapperton was the most accomplished member, opened up the Lake Chad region and much of the basin of the lower Niger. During a second expedition on which Clapperton died, his companions, the brothers Lander, traced the Niger to its unsuspected outlet through the so-called Oil Rivers, numerous small streams reaching the sea through a wide, swampy delta. Although much important information was added subsequently, notably by such men as Dr. Heinrich Barth (1851-1855) and Paul du Chaillu (1856-1868), the great northwestern portion of Africa was comprehended in the main by the beginning of the reign of Queen Victoria in 1837.

These and a host of other exploits no less daring and scarcely less eventful made Africa the laboratory of the missionary, the scientist and the explorer during the second half of the nineteenth century. Thus far the continent had been penetrated principally from the north and west, water courses usually directing the routes of march. The dawning interest created by these enterprises was greatly stimulated by a new series of explorations starting from the east and south coasts and still following the water courses. In 1858 Richard Burton and John Speke discovered Lake Tanganyika, and Speke and James A. Grant in 1862 supplemented this with the discovery of one of the sources of the Nile in Victoria Nyanza. Profiting from these experiences, Sir Samuel Baker in 1864 discovered another source of the Nile in Albert Nyanza and investigated the eastern Sudan. But the culmination of this period of exploration was reached in the remarkable work of the missionary-explorer, David Livingstone, and in the more spectacular exploits of his successor, Henry M. Stanley. It was the accomplishments of these men in particular which gave rise to an unparalleled wave of popular fascination and entailed results of the most profound nature.

Livingstone, who more than any one else may be credited with the final unveiling of Africa, had prepared for life as a missionary. But, prone to investigate, he left family and friends and assumed a roving commission soon after his arrival in Bechuanaland in 1840. Ministering to the natives as he went, he discovered Lake Ngami in 1849 and reached the Zambesi River in 1851. In 1853 he traced the upper Zambesi to its source and thence pushed across the watershed to the West Coast at St. Paul de Loanda. Retracing his steps the following year, he followed the Zambesi through what was later named Rhodesia, reaching the East Coast in 1856, an exploit which immediately attracted world-wide attention and determined his later career. He formally relinquished the rôle of missionary for that of explorer in 1858 and explored the lower Zambesi, the Shiré River and Lake Nyasa while the sources of the Nile were being discovered by his countrymen.

Livingstone's last journey, starting from Zanzibar in 1866, was inspired by the doubt still remaining concerning the affluents of the great eastern lakes. During the next few years he surveyed much of upper Rhodesia, discovering new lakes and various sources of the Congo River, which he believed to be tributaries of the Nile. The prolonged absence of news from him on this occasion created widespread anxiety and gave rise to the relief expedition led by Henry M. Stanley, which located Livingstone on Lake Tanganyika in 1871.

Upon the latter's death two years later, the cloak of primacy in Central African exploration fell upon Stanley. It was this Elisha of African exploration who carried through and largely popularized the spade work of Livingstone and his contemporary, Lovett Cameron. Working under a joint commission from the *New York Herald* and the London *Daily Telegraph*, Stanley was commissioned in 1874 "to solve, if possible, the remaining problems of the geography of Central Africa, and to investigate and report upon the haunts of the slave-traders." Setting out from the island of Zanzibar in November, 1874, Stanley devoted nearly two years to a thorough survey of the great lake region of eastern Central Africa. Then embarking on the much-debated Lualaba River near its source in Lake Bangweolo, he alone of several Europeans survived the extremely perilous descent to prove that it was indeed not the Nile, as Livingstone believed, but the Congo.

Stanley's identification of the Congo in 1877 marks the close of the first period of African exploration. The main features of the continent by that time had been roughly sketched in and a partial inventory both of natural resources and of natural obstacles had been taken. Only the supplementary work of Stanley, supported by the King of the Belgians, and of the distinguished French agent and explorer, Savorgnan de Brazza, along the Congo and its tributaries was needed to suggest to European chancelleries the advantages of territorial acquisitions. The revelations of Livingstone concerning the nature and vast extent of the slave traffic maintained by the Arabs over wide areas provided a ready means whereby interested European governments might tentatively assume certain responsibilities in Africa without prematurely arousing a suspicion that they harbored ulterior motives. Within a decade from the end of Livingstone's career, the scramble for Africa had definitely begun with Stanley and De Brazza as principal agents, and in another decade almost the entire continent had been appropriated.

### THE CONGO AND THE BERLIN CONFERENCE

The partition of Africa by European states as a process began early in the nineteenth century with English penetration into the interior from the Cape of Good Hope and with French expansion in Senegal and Algeria. As a movement, it commenced with the action of King Leopold II of Belgium in assembling at Brussels in September, 1876, representatives from seven European states for a "geographical conference." Prior to this time, the Powers had generally avoided acquiring possessions in a distant continent of poor repute beyond such as promised immediate, definite and material advantages. Leopold certainly did not guess that he was about to usher in an era of intense colonial competition, but he did propose to "open to civilization the only part of our globe where it has not yet penetrated."

At his instance, the conference of 1876 formed an International African Association under his guidance and provided for the establishment of affiliated branches in the principal European countries and in the United States. By the time this machinery was ready to function for purposes presumably altruistic, Leopold's interest was drawn from East Africa, where his gaze had first rested, to the Congo basin by the remarkable exploits of Stanley. Before the explorer's return to Europe in 1878, he had been selected as the chief agent of the Association in carrying out its program. As an Englishman, Stanley desired a commission from his own country; but when that was denied him he accepted a mandate from Leopold as secret agent of a special section of the Association, the *Comité d'Études du Haut Congo,* or Committee for the Study of the Upper Congo.

The hundreds of treaties Stanley obtained from Bantu chiefs in Central Africa between August, 1879, and August, 1884, whereby they recognized the protective authority of the *Comité d'Études,* took special note of the commercial possibilities of the region. But the cat was already out of the bag and Stanley was not in time to forestall similar activities of Count de Brazza, whose first explorations in the lower Congo basin were contemporary with those of Stanley. By clever sparring, however, territorial claims of the French were confined to the northern shore of the river. The expense of Congo exploration, the rival spirit displayed by various national branches, and his own unrevealed motives led Leopold in 1882 to transform the International African Association, including the *Comité d'Études,* into a centralized International Association of the Congo which did not conceal its commercial object.

The penetration of France within the Congo basin and the rapidly changing character of the International Association could not but arouse Great Britain and Portugal. The former was unwilling, under a Liberal Government, to acquire any new commitments in Africa. Portugal, however, had for a great while claimed the West Coast as far north as 5° 12' S., that is, both sides of the mouth of the Congo and inland indefinitely. Since 1846 she had tried repeatedly, but in vain, to secure formal recognition of these claims from Great Britain. But it was now remembered in England that Portugal had for centuries been a commercial ally and that Portuguese colonies were rapidly becoming British wards. In view of these considerations, an Anglo-Portuguese Convention was concluded February 26, 1884, recognizing Portuguese sovereignty over the mouth of the Congo and providing for Anglo-Portuguese control of navigation on the river.

The treaty was furiously assailed. France considered it a direct affront. The Germans complained that "Africa is a large pudding which the English have prepared for themselves at other people's expense, and the crust of which is already fit for eating." English of all parties accused their government of having made an iniquitous bargain in extending the range of power of a state so incompetent and corrupt in colonial administration. Even in Portugal the treaty was unpopular. The French and German governments, conscious for once of similar interests and sentiments, formally protested. Bismarck then seized upon a Portuguese suggestion for an international conference and, with French coöperation, issued invitations to almost all of the European nations and to the United States to consider at Berlin freedom of trade in the Congo basin, freedom of navigation on the Congo and Niger Rivers, and the rules to be observed in the future occupation of African territories. The discussion of such a program under the auspices of Germany and France, both of whom were busily furthering their own ends in Africa, was unpalatable, particularly to Great Britain, but the proposal was everywhere accepted.

Before the Conference opened, its labors were simplified to a degree by the voluntary scrapping of the Anglo-Portuguese Convention and the partial recognition of the International Association of the Congo as an independent state. The Conference therefore devoted its labors, not so much to the moral issues featured in Bismarck's opening address, as to questions affecting trade and land titles.

The General Act of the Conference, signed on February 26, 1885, undertook to regularize the African contest already well under way by laying down general rules designed to avert dangerous clashes. It typified the new imperialism in that it recognized the right of Europeans to extend their control over African peoples regardless of race or existing institutions and confined its humanitarian provisions to a general denunciation of slavery and the slave trade. In order to solve existing difficulties, Portugal, although receiving territory on both sides of the Congo, was denied control of the mouth of that river and the Congo Free State was erected under the "enlightened" sovereignty of King Leopold. But the Conference thought to keep the Congo economically international by providing for a scheme of neutrality and by creating a commission to maintain freedom of trade and navigation. However, since no means of financing or empowering the commission was devised, the Congo Free State became free in name only.

For the future the Conference set up a kind of international code of ethics by decreeing that no Power should establish a new protectorate in Africa without first giving due notice of the intent, that recognition of territorial claims must depend on effective occupation, and that disputes were to be settled by arbitration. These, doubtless, were wise provisions; but in the absence of any permanent international organization or other supervising agency the General Act served more as an ideal than as a legislative enactment in the contests that followed.

### EVOLUTION OF THE BELGIAN CONGO

The ink was scarcely dry on the General Act of the Berlin Conference before the King of the Congo Free State began employing his new and practically unrestricted authority. He declared the neutrality of his state, speeded up the work of exploration and boundary delimitation, and effected the destruction of Arab power at the headwaters of the Congo. At the same time, all lands not actually occupied or under cultivation were nationalized, amounting to nearly half of the entire area of more than 900,000 square miles.

At an early date Leopold recognized the desirability of having no foreign "stockholders" as possible critics of his Congo enterprise. In 1887 he bought out all non-Belgian interests, and the Congo ceased to be international in any real sense.  Leopold presently reimbursed himself by reserving a crown district, ten times the size of Belgium, of the richest rubber lands. Here, as elsewhere in the Congo, special monopolies for the exploitation of natural products, including rights of native labor, were awarded from time to time to commercial concerns in most of which Leopold was a heavy stockholder.  His profits, therefore, were derived both from the stipends paid to the state by the concessionaires and from the dividends earned in the course of their immensely successful operations.

Thus, with a fine disregard for the spirit of the original Congo organization and the provisions of the Berlin Conference, the Congo basin became a closed country and a system of forced labor replaced but scarcely improved upon the technical slavery in vogue when the region was first opened up for "civilizing" purposes.  It is probable that the resources of the Congo, however extensive, could not have been profitably exploited in any other way at the outset.  In a tropical, disease-ridden country wholly unsuited for European labor, inhabited by numerous savages and altogether lacking in highways except those supplied by tortuous river channels, it was inevitable that on any but a purely altruistic basis the white man's boasted civilization would not appear to advantage. But the evils inherent in the situation were considerably aggravated by other factors.  First, there was the necessity of quickly proving "effective occupation" of a very large area in order to insure its possession.  Another source of trouble lay in the peculiar nature of the Congo state, which, concentrated in the person of

Leopold, lacked both the economic stability of a nation and the regulating influence of its public sentiment. And beyond these were the utter irresponsibility and unchecked greed of the concessionaires.

Under such a system, the exactions laid on native villages tended to increase as larger profits became more certain. To increase production and to supplement their own meagre stipends, company and state officials resorted to the most cruel and abusive treatment of natives, and from this the natives had no recourse. Whole areas eventually were desolated, denuded alike of native populations and marketable products.

The leavening influence of an aroused public conscience in Europe, long delayed by careful censorship and rigorous exclusion from the Congo, at last became manifest. By 1890 reports were going into circulation concerning breaches of the Berlin Act in the Congo. The native issue was taken up in 1893 in England by the Aborigines Protection Society. The British press began championing the black man's cause in 1901, and two years later the British Government began an official opposition to the administration of the Congo which lasted until after Belgian annexation. Other governments, including that of the United States, fell into line. The timely publication of books and reports by explorers, missionaries and consular officials immensely widened the scope of interest. The multiplication of reform associations bore witness to the growth of a world conscience and popular interest in world affairs.

In 1896 the Congo Government, as a gesture to its

critics, appointed an innocuous commission to provide for native protection. But by 1905 the rising clamor demanded something more substantial, and a Commission of Inquiry was appointed to report on conditions existing in the Congo. The Commission's report, while partially suppressed, was still sufficiently condemnatory to elicit promises of far-reaching reforms from the sovereign. Already Leopold realized that grave evils were inherent in a régime dependent for its income on a tropical African possession. The natural solution was that placed by the King before the Belgian Parliament in June, 1906—the annexation of the Congo Free State and the erection under a colonial ministry of a complete administrative system based on a program of gradual development rather than of exploitation. The Belgian Government, reflecting the absence of imperialistic sentiment in the country, was slow to act, but after extended negotiations with the King, the Congo Free State became a Belgian colony on November 15, 1908.

This transfer of sovereignty was not an immediate panacea for Congo ills. The Great Powers were variously minded about the legality of the transfer: the German Empire, for example, recognized the new status at once, while Great Britain formally sanctioned it only in 1913 after various concessionaire companies had lost their charters. Although a Colonial Council was added to the Belgian Government, few improvements were effected in the administration of the colony until after the death of Leopold in December, 1909. Colonial reform was speeded up during the early reign of his successor, Albert, because of the personal knowledge and sympathy of the King himself, the growing influence of the Belgian Socialist Party, the increasing revelation of the extent to which the Congo had been "milked dry" by the concessionaires, and the realization that the future value of the region would depend on a careful development of both native populations and industries.

In pursuance of the new policy, the blacks were emancipated from the virtual slavery of the previous system, given local civil rights, and, in 1913, granted free lands for cultivation as they pleased. Arbitrary and cruel acts of colonial officials, made punishable, rapidly decreased. Taxation was completely revised. To take the place of the exhausted trade in ivory and native rubber, mineral deposits, especially of copper, gold and diamonds, and palm products were developed. Recent experiments in the cultivation of cotton, rice and cocoa have promised well. And since 1914 railway and road construction have become a significant feature of a new era.

These changes and improvements, however, have entailed a heavy cost. Pure exploitation is said to have netted King Leopold a fortune of twenty million dollars. His concessionaires amassed many millions more. Congo development, requiring larger administrative staffs, improved communications, and a material growth based on voluntary labor, has produced only heavy deficits. The labor problem is perhaps most difficult of all, and its solution—if a solution there be— lies in the education of the natives' needs and desires which they may be willing to satisfy through the medium of labor. But in spite of the handicaps, the

steady annual increase of Congo trade and the spirit
of the Belgian people are good auguries for the future.

## THE FRENCH RÉGIME IN TUNIS

While Leopold of Belgium was industriously evolv-
ing schemes for Central Africa and infecting the European Powers with covetous excitement, France was con-
tributing considerably to the growth of an imperialistic
state of mind in Europe by fastening her hold on Tunis.
This section of North Africa, adjoining Algeria on the
east, had come under Turkish control in the sixteenth
century, but had achieved virtual independence under
its own line of beys early in the eighteenth. France
had obtained special concessions in this regency at the
time of the attack on Algiers, and other European nations hastened to follow suit. Italians, in particular,
eyed Tunis as a sphere for future national activity.

As in Algeria, internal conditions furnished a basis
for European intervention. A change of régime was
inevitable from the time when the Bey of Tunis suc-
cumbed to the temptation of borrowing large sums of
money abroad at high rates of interest and without regard to future repayment or to the effects on his pov-
erty-stricken subjects of increasing taxes. Suspension
of interest payments on loans and the extent of French
investments involved led the French Government in
1869 to undertake the supervision of the Bey's finances.
The instant protests of Great Britain and Italy resulted
in a joint financial commission of these Powers and a
period of heated rivalry in which each state attempted
to secure for its nationals a major share in the development of Tunisian resources. Meanwhile, a constant

source of trouble had arisen in the interior of the regency, where rebellious Algerian tribesmen habitually retreated across the Tunisian border, whence they might raid the Algerian hinterland with impunity. The unwillingness or inability of the Bey to end these disturbances or even to prevent his own tribesmen from joining in the forays gave rise to a long series of French grievances and at last provided the occasion for armed intervention.

Such action as France might have taken immediately to supersede the joint commission and to extend political or financial control over Tunis was considerably delayed by the Franco-German War. French preoccupation and defeat played directly into the hands of colonial rivals and contributed largely to Italy's growing belief in her Tunisian heritage. But the fate of Tunis, long before marked for European exploitation, was settled less with regard to primacy of European interests in the regency itself than to the exigencies of statecraft in Europe. In 1878 the Congress of Berlin, meeting to reconsider the Turkish Question, was forced to countenance the coincident Anglo-Turkish Convention, which accorded to Great Britain the control of the island of Cyprus. The territorial readjustment elsewhere made necessary by this move included a quiet suggestion to France that her compensation might be found in Tunis. Such an arrangement appealed to Bismarck as likely to create in Italy an enemy to France and an ally for the Central Powers. It was approved by Disraeli as most likely to counteract French indignation at the British occupation of Cyprus.

The Italians, ignorant of the bargain, meanwhile took advantage of high favor with the Bey to secure desirable concessions in the regency. Their purchase of a railway from British interests in 1880, inconsiderable in itself, roused the French Government to the point of carrying out the program already sanctioned at Berlin. A series of timely incidents on the border between Tunis and Algeria and the refusal of the Italophile Bey to make any amends gave the occasion for an armed punitive expedition. With little thought of the difficulties and sacrifices entailed in the expedition to Algiers in 1830, a large French army was sent into Tunis from the west in April, 1881, while a French fleet was despatched to operate along the coast. On May 12, the Bey, having failed to secure aid from his suzerain or from any of the Powers which had lately guaranteed the integrity of the Turkish dominions, capitulated completely and signed the Treaty of Bardo. This, while continuing his dynasty, made him for the future a French ward by placing his country permanently under the protection of France.

It required no little care to quiet the furor aroused by this, one of the first definite moves in what was to be known as the partition of Africa. The British Government, then in the hands of the Liberals, protested vigorously against the action. The Italian Government, true to Bismarck's expectations, immediately entered the Triple Alliance and planned that vengeance which is not yet entirely forgotten.

However, by guaranteeing all existing treaties with Tunis and avoiding the costly errors made during the early years of the Algerian enterprise, the French régime was soon established on a permanent basis and an era of political tranquillity and economic prosperity was inaugurated. Much of this evolution has been ascribed to the wisdom of the French Foreign Office. More surely it has been due to the natural advantages of the country, which, more than any other portion of North Africa, is fitted for European colonization. An ingenious, if not wholly satisfactory, scheme has been instituted for naturalizing as French citizens the alien European inhabitants, most of whom are Italians. Commercially, Tunis bids fair to become a really profitable venture. Trade has increased twenty-five hundred per cent since the beginning of French control, and the application of high tariffs since 1896 has more than repaid the costs of occupation and development.

In the course of this growth, several governmental changes have been made, principally with a view to bringing all essential features of administration under French control, while leaving local institutions largely in the hands of caids and sheikhs. Representation in legislative councils of various grades has been successfully introduced. Tunisia remains technically a protectorate, although with good reason it is generally considered as little different in status from the older colony of Algeria, which is an integral part of the French state.

A most significant result of improving administration in both provinces has been the loyalty with which the sedentary and even the nomadic tribesmen have supported the French Government in time of need. The skill with which the French have coped with the demands of various elements in the colonial population, particularly since the World War, may offer some justi-

fication for European imperialism. Theirs is not an
empty boast that they have performed "a sacred duty,
which a superior civilization contracts toward less advanced peoples."

### BUILDING OF THE FRENCH WEST AFRICAN EMPIRE

It has already been noted that early European contacts with Africa were confined mainly to the West
Coast in the interests of the slave trade, and that when
this trade was abolished the European factories fell into
a state of desuetude. These early contacts left none
but evil results, yet it was here that European nations
made most rapid headway in the nineteenth century.

Commercial activity in Africa after the Napoleonic
Wars was not confined, as it had been earlier, to scattered fringes of the coast. Vast technical improvements and vast capital resources now made possible
extended experiments into the truth of the mercantile
dictum that "trade follows the flag." The French,
probably because of the lack, after 1815, of other out-
lets for national energy, first elected to test the truth
of this doctrine in the interior of West Africa.

While the hinterland of Algeria was being conquered
in the north, tentative probings into the interior were
made from the French bases in Senegambia. By 1865
French authority had already been established over
some hundreds of square miles, but the real vision of
African possibilities did not appear to French imperialists until near the beginning of the eighteen eighties.
Then, having renewed connections with some old trading posts north of the Mellicouri River, on the Ivory
Coast, at Porto Novo in Dahomey, along the Gabun

River and on the north bank of the Congo, the glamor-
ous idea took shape of a French West African empire
stretching from Algeria to the Congo and from the
Senegal to the Nile or even to the Red Sea.  It formed
the more rapidly because of the increasing activity of
the British, the German penchant for creating protectorates by means of armed cruisers, and the wholesale
operations of the Belgian *Comité d'Études*.   The
French did not wait to count the cost of their colonial
program; the great problem was the establishment of
"effective occupation" wherever possible.

A principal obstacle to the realization of the French
ideal lay in the numerous rival holdings along the
West Coast between Cape Verde and the Congo.  As
these had been acquired in the first place because of
their strategic positions and commercial possibilities,
they naturally served as bases for the tapping of the
resources of the interior.  It therefore became French
strategy to outflank these rivals in a race for the hinterland.  Want of space precludes even a mention of the
many expeditions by which this purpose was carried
out.  However, by 1884 De Brazza's contest with Stanley had expanded the station of Gabun into the great
French Congo protectorate.  On the Niger, the key position of Timbuktu and the native kingdoms in the
great bend of the river had been acquired by 1895.
But the determination to secure an outlet by way of
the lower Niger was foiled by British precautions, and
in the Anglo-French Convention of June 14, 1898, this
field was abandoned to the British Royal Niger Company.

By the late nineties France had made notable progress in consolidating her West African holdings. The strips of coast line that had possessed only local significance fifteen years before were now the doors through which an immense hinterland reached the outer world. The coastal stations which had appeared as serious rivals at the outset remained in most cases merely enclaves in French territory. Only British Nigeria and German Kamerun reached far enough into the interior to possess the elements of permanent stability. Even the attempts of the British and Germans to prevent the junction of the French Congo with French West Africa by extending their holdings to Lake Chad did not prevent the geographical union of French territories by way of the Sahara and the Western Sudan.

The penetration of the Sudan was a most ambitious undertaking, in view of its vast extent and great distance from French bases. Yet this was deemed advisable as a means of linking up the Congo territories with the West Coast through the Sahara as well as providing an outlet by way of the Nile for the interior provinces. The valuable Bahr-el-Ghazal district, since 1885 in the hands of the Mahdists, was entered in 1896. The story of Major Marchand's expedition to Fashoda on the Nile is familiar—his clash with the English in September, 1898, and the agreement reached on March 21, 1899. While this was not wholly satisfactory to France, still it constituted a formal recognition of French sovereignty over the spacious western Sudan.

Only some portions of the Sahara were needed to round out the long coveted empire. The western portion had already been entered by sundry expeditions both from Algeria and from the West Coast. The remaining oases were now quickly visited and the fierce desert tribes brought within the French sphere. Effective occupation naturally followed more slowly, yet civil government has now been set up over most of the Sahara and the lawlessness of the desert has given way, except in the most remote regions, to a fair degree of security. Thus the French dream of a North African empire has been abundantly realized.

Much of French Africa is of real value. Trade here has followed the flag. The eight colonies comprising French West Africa, having an annual trade of a billion francs or more, promise an economic justification of the cost of acquisition. The rise of a great port and imperial city on Cape Verde at Dakar, the rapid extension of means of communication, and thriving and contented native populations are indications of the success of French imperialism. Yet these and other material developments, however gratifying, do not represent the bounds of French satisfaction in contemplating their work in Africa, for national pride cannot be weighed in material scales.

### THE BRITISH IN WEST AFRICA

The few small British trading concerns operating in West Africa when the territorial scramble began were poorly equipped to compete, as they were compelled to, with the French and Germans. Whereas traders from the Continent came as official or unofficial agents of their governments, the Islanders had to rely wholly on their own efforts. The British houses on the lower

Niger would have failed even to survive but for the timely efforts of an ex-officer, Sir George Goldie. His foresight in bringing the independent Niger merchants in 1879 into a United African Company, soon renamed the National African Company, created a capital sufficiently large to make possible a vigorous trade war with their rivals. French concerns were already established on the river for more than purely commercial reasons, but in 1884 the English had the satisfaction of forcing them out and obtaining a monopolistic control of the entire lower Niger basin. It was this accomplished fact, recognized by the British Government on the very eve of the Berlin Conference, which foiled Bismarck's patent intent of having the whole Niger valley declared an open field for commercial exploitation.

The middle course of the Niger still remained unappropriated. Here the British had to contend with both Germans and French, who frequently resorted to stealth to accomplish their purposes. A characteristic German *coup* was undertaken by the German African and Colonial Societies in 1885 by sending out a merchant to make overtures to the great native kingdoms of the middle Niger. But the National African Company, apprised of the German scheme, had the immense satisfaction of bringing these native states under their protection before the arrival of the German mission. The British Government thereupon established a protectorate over the whole of the Niger Coast westward to the old colony of Lagos, and in 1886, with the accession of the Salisbury Ministry, the National African Company secured a charter as the Royal Niger Company and embarked on an era of prosperous growth. Its operations were not uncontested, for until the Anglo-French treaty of 1898 unrelaxing vigilance and some physical force were necessary to check the constant stream of French expeditions coming down from the upper Niger and overland from the West Coast and to maintain a hinterland sufficient for the Company's commercial needs.

By the end of the nineteenth century, the Company's work as an imperial agency was finished. In a style characteristic of imperial expansion in undeveloped countries, its political functions were taken over by the Crown in 1900 in return for adequate compensation. With this a more advanced stage of colonial development began, leading to the organization of the whole of Nigeria, including the colony and protectorate of Lagos, into a single political sphere in 1914. In British West Africa the flag has followed trade.

The other British holdings in West Africa, though never so closely pressed, failed to keep pace with the growth of Nigeria. The Gambia settlement, the oldest British possession in Africa, perhaps progressed least. Long after the ending of the slave trade, Gambia remained subject to the government of Sierra Leone. In 1888 it received the dignity of a separate government, but at the completion of its growth in 1891 it included only the navigable portion of the Gambia River. Sierra Leone, once the keystone of the West African settlements, fared little better. The annals of the Gold Coast are not so brief. As a result of a treaty made in 1828 by the merchant rulers of the Gold Coast, the British Crown, which assumed control in 1843, had frequent troubles with the King of the Ashanti. A series of campaigns between 1873 and 1900 led to the creation of two new protectorates, one over the Ashanti proper and another over the Northern Territories, all now under one jurisdiction.

These three colonies offer good illustrations of certain successive stages in the establishment of European dominion. They originated in the operations of chartered trading monopolies, which, having completed the pioneer work, surrendered their political powers into the hands of the Crown. The coastal sections then became true Crown colonies, directly ruled by nominated executive and legislative councils and presided over by governors, who also ruled by indirect means the protectorate zones beyond. But still further inland, where spheres of influence normally would have sprung up, is French domain and the natural lines of economic flow have been diverted, leaving the British colonies mere enclaves. The old West Coast settlements, therefore, with the exception of Lagos, which, as a parasite, derives sustenance from its host, Nigeria, remain in a state of arrested development—too firmly established to perish and yet without the means of vigorous life. In a way, it may be said that the creation of the French colonial empire in West Africa has been at the expense of the British.

## THE GERMANS IN WEST AND SOUTHWEST AFRICA

Although the flag of Brandenburg had briefly appeared on the Guinea Coast late in the seventeenth century, there were no natural impulses to an appreciable widening of the German horizon for two centuries to come. *Laissez faire* was both an economic and a political watchword. But at last a definite change was wrought by the Industrial Revolution and by political unification, and the energies thus created found release in national expansion.

Prince Bismarck, creator of the German Empire, had hard shift to restrain premature expressions of national imperialism while giving encouragement to the growth of commerce. However, the early eighteen eighties found him partially converted, either by persuasion or necessity, to all the elements of a program of colonial expansion. Up to this time, European penetration into Africa had been proceeding slowly and without marked rivalry. But the establishment of France in Algeria and Tunis, Great Britain in South Africa and Egypt, and the International Congo Association in Central Africa had already produced new strains and stresses. By the time the Berlin Conference had completed its labors, Germany had staked out a colonial empire of more than a million square miles containing some ten million inhabitants.

The opening of the new dispensation was marked by a series of unostentatious but significant events affecting the west coast of Africa. At several points, notably in the region of the Kamerun River, German merchants had previously negotiated treaties with native chiefs whereby these placed themselves under German protection. In 1883 a Bremen merchant, Herr F. A. E. Lüderitz, under promise of government protection, effected the purchase of a relatively small tract of territory adjacent to the port of Angra Pequeña in Southwest Africa. Early in the following year the

noted explorer, Dr. Gustav Nachtigal, was despatched
to the African coast in a warship with instructions to
take possession of such regions as remained unclaimed,
including Angra Pequeña. His first act was the occupation of Little Popo Island in the Gulf of Guinea.
Then, taking advantage of a disputed native succession
on the coast opposite, he claimed the entire region for
Germany and thus laid the basis for the colony of
Togoland. Proceeding southward, the Kamerun district was next added. This barely forestalled a British
expedition on a similar errand, but it did not prevent
the preëmption by the British of the Oil Rivers in the
Niger delta. The work of Lüderitz and Nachtigal was
full of deep meaning with respect to the changed policy
of the German Government and the type of diplomacy
which was to characterize the imperialistic period just
dawning, but this was not everywhere perceived. Other
and more forceful lessons were near at hand.

The southwest portion of the African coast had long
been considered by the British as their own special
sphere of influence. Sections of the interior had already been annexed to prevent occupation by the Boers,
and other portions were marked for early occupation.
In 1878 Walfish Bay and a small section dependent
thereon had been annexed by the Cape Colony, but the
Cape Government was unwilling at that time to assume
control of the whole region south of Angola. In 1880
the German Government asked British protection for
the hard pressed German missions in Namaqualand,
but the Gladstone Ministry refused to assume any
definite responsibility. In February, 1883, the British
Government was asked whether it would extend pro-

tection to a Bremen merchant (Lüderitz) who was about to set up a factory on the southwest coast. Again an evasive answer was returned, on the ground that such matters pertained to the Cape Government. But after the German purchase of Angra Pequeña, Lord Granville, British Foreign Minister, pointed out that "any claim to sovereignty or jurisdiction by a foreign power between the southern point of Portuguese jurisdiction at latitude 18° and the frontier of Cape Colony would infringe upon [British] legitimate rights," and at the same time urged the Cape Government to extend its control over the region in question. Party difficulties and the dread of expense postponed action on the matter, and it was only on July 23, 1884, that the Cape Parliament, in a fit of anxiety, voted to annex Angra Pequeña. But it was already too late. Long out of patience with British dilatoriness, Bismarck had authorized the announcement of a German protectorate over Lüderitzland on April 24.

Faced with this *fait accompli*, British authorities gave up their first intent of contesting the move and with an air of good sportsmanship welcomed the Germans as colonial neighbors, nevertheless reserving their post at Walfish Bay and various islands along the coast. A joint commission of adjustment, reporting in 1886, awarded to Germany not merely the few thousand square miles of Lüderitzland but a huge region, embracing about a fourth of the continent south of the Zambesi River. A supplementary arrangement in 1890 added still further to the protectorate by conceding an outlet to the Zambesi for the hinterland. Other leading

Powers, with their eyes fixed on other territories, had little criticism for these bargains.

In pursuing a career as a colonizing power, the German Empire soon demonstrated the impossibility of borrowing extensively from the experience of nations longer in the field. At the outset it was handicapped by the absence of colonial machinery, a lack of trained and experienced men, ignorance of the resources and physical limitations of the territories acquired, and by a misunderstanding of the natives. Each of these produced its own train of unfortunate consequences. Substantial progress was delayed for several years by leaving the administration of colonial territories to concessionaire companies, whose only concern was to exploit their holdings for quick returns. The colonial outlook was improved when, in 1890, the Colonial Department of the Foreign Office was created, but it was only after the assumption of direct imperial responsibility and the establishment of the Colonial Office in 1907 that rapid and consistent headway was made toward colonial success.

The development of Southwest Africa involved difficulties of a unique character. With Walfish Bay, the natural outlet of the region, in British hands, it was necessary to construct another, though less adequate, harbor at Swakopmund. The light rainfall, the absence of water for irrigation, and the prevalence of animal pests made agriculture and stock raising difficult even in the better sections. The great Kalahari Desert offered few advantages of any kind. To these more or less permanent handicaps was added an almost fatal disaster in the uprising of the Herreros in 1904. These difficulties were all exceedingly costly in lives and money, but at least they disclosed to the Germans many new phases of the colonial problem and led to wholesale improvements.

A basis of prosperity in Southwest Africa at last was found in extensive and valuable mineral deposits. Small quantities of gold and abundant sources of tin, copper, silver and lead, together with the rapid development of electrical energy, went far toward compensating for the lack of rainfall. Yet the principal source of wealth lay in extensive diamond fields. These resources and the rapid extension of railway lines made Southwest Africa a land of considerable promise before the World War, though permanent white settlers were few.

Meanwhile, German footholds in West Africa had attained their maximum growth. Togoland, thrust vigorously as a wedge between the British Gold Coast (Ashanti) and French Dahomey, was destined to remain a narrow enclave. The Kamerun, however, with boundaries undefined for several years, found opportunity for extensive growth. The Anglo-German Agreement of 1890 provided for an outlet to Lake Chad on the northeast, while the settlement of the Moroccan dispute with France twenty years later extended the colony on the southeast to the Congo and its tributaries at two points.

In physical and climatic conditions, resources, and problems of development, Togoland and Kamerun offer complete contrasts with Southwest Africa. While their development under German management was in

most respects satisfactory, they remained so back-
ward that the German Colonial Office was willing to
offer them to France in 1911 for a share of Morocco.
In both colonies the Germans experimented with
native education, particularly with regard to health
and sanitation, with some slight success. Some economic returns were obtained, not only from the
ubiquitous palm products and rubber, but from scientific forestry in valuable woods, such as teak and ma-
hogany, and even from cattle and cotton. The progress made along these lines did much to counteract
the early mistakes in administration and to place Germany in a relatively high position as a colonizing
Power. It has remained for Great Britain and France
as mandatories to reap most of the advantages from
this pioneering work.

## THE CONTEST FOR EAST AFRICA

The division of East Africa into spheres and protectorates followed from much the same causes as
those which brought about the partition of the western
part of the continent. Until 1884 European nations
had generally avoided acquiring territorial responsibilities along the East Coast. Portugal, to be sure,
had maintained a weak position in Mozambique since
the early part of the sixteenth century and France
cherished nominal claims in Madagascar. But such
authority as existed along the East Coast from the
Gulf of Aden to Mozambique was mostly in the hands
of the Sultans of Zanzibar.

Zanzibar is geographically, politically and commercially the pivotal position for the whole of east cen-

tral Africa.  British influence, first implanted here in
1861 by the Viceroy of India, was afterward system-
atically cultivated by a political agent, Dr. John Kirk,
who came to exercise almost dictatorial power.  On
more than one occasion he was prepared to deliver a
large part of East Africa politically and economically
into British hands, only to be snubbed by the British
Foreign Office for his pains.

Meanwhile, commercially minded Germans had been
observing the potentialities of East Africa since 1844.
The completion of the Suez Canal inspired something
more than commercial interest in German minds and
the completion of German unification in 1871 provided
the necessary means for a new type of German enterprise.  In 1877 the German Colonial Society was
founded, followed by the German African Society in
1878.  But these organizations were not aggressive
enough for such active spirits as Dr. Karl Peters,
Count J. F. Pheil and others, who in 1884 formed
a new Society for German Colonization with definite
political objectives in East Africa.

Bismarck's usual hostility to projects for German
colonial expansion does not appear in his relations
with the new society.  Doubtless he was intrigued by
the peculiar opportunities of the moment, the British
being preoccupied with a Sudan campaign and Russian
advances in Central Asia, the French being absorbed
with Tunis, and the rules under consideration by the
Berlin Conference not yet formulated.  At any rate,
no serious obstacles were placed in the way of the offi-
cers of the Colonization Society, who quietly slipped
out to East Africa and contracted a dozen treaties with

credulous native chiefs which ceded outright an area
of some 60,000 square miles on the mainland to German interests.

About the same time and significantly, Dr. Gerhard
Rohlfs, of Sahara exploration fame, was despatched on
an armed cruiser to serve as German Consul-General
at Zanzibar. English alarm at these developments
caused the Foreign Office tactfully to inquire concerning German intentions in this British sphere.
Bismarck's petulant reply explained little, but it was
found satisfactory by the Liberal Ministry. The British surrender was apparently complete. Consul-General Kirk was instructed to coöperate with Rohlfs as
far as possible—a command which threw into the dis-
card most of his life's work. Thus are patriots some-
times rewarded.

Bismarck still hesitated entirely to abandon his
anti-imperialistic policy. It was only when Peters
threatened to transfer the East African holdings of the
Colonization Society to the Belgian Crown that, early
in March, 1885, a *Schutzbrief* was issued taking them
under German protection. Sultan Barghash of Zanzibar, whose extensive possessions on the mainland were
thus being preëmpted, was still to be reckoned with.
Abetted by Kirk, he was about to undertake a military
campaign into the affected zone when the arrival of
a German naval squadron in the neighborhood of his
capital compelled him to acquiesce in the late arrangements.

Still all was not lost for the British in East Africa.
While Dr. Peters was assiduously concluding treaties
west of Zanzibar, an English explorer, Sir Harry John-

ston, was carrying on similar activities in the neighborhood of Mt. Kilimanjaro. His work became the basis
for the organization in 1885 of the British East Africa
Association, later incorporated as the Imperial British
East Africa Company.

The rules lately adopted at Berlin, French claims,
and the rival activities of British and Germans all
called for a delimitation of interests in East Africa.
Late in 1885 the three Powers most concerned created
for that purpose an "impartial Commission," which
announced its findings in June of the following year.
Sultan Barghash was permitted to retain Zanzibar,
Pemba and dependent islands and to continue as sovereign of a strip of mainland coast ten miles wide and
about a thousand miles long, together with a few additional stations. The back country, by a separate
agreement, was made into two zones, the smaller northern one passing to Great Britain, the southern to
Germany. The French were satisfied with the recognition of their claims in Madagascar. The settlement
was completed by British and German leases of the
Sultan's coastal territory adjacent to their protectorates.

Now that competition for African territory was in
full swing, the Anglo-German contest shifted to a new
area. According to the accepted principles of European imperialism, the region of Uganda, a fertile, attractive, upland country controlling the headwaters of
the Nile, was suitable ground for European enterprise.
Partially explored years before, this Negro kingdom
had since become the scene of the most jealous prose-
lyting activities on the part of English Protestant,

French Catholic and Mohammedan sectaries. Their rivalries had produced a state of civil war, during which the restoration of King Mwanga to a precarious throne in October, 1889, coincided with a new venture of Dr. Karl Peters, aimed at securing German influence in this attractive region.

Under guise of effecting the rescue of a German officer from the Mahdists in the Sudan, Peters evaded the watchful British, reached Uganda, and obtained a doubtful treaty from Mwanga on March 1, 1890. This resulted in no tangible gain, though it may have given the German officials greater bargaining power in the important negotiations which ensued. Already overtures had been made to Great Britain by the German Government looking toward a readjustment of African claims and boundaries on the basis of the German acquisition of the island of Heligoland in the North Sea, needed as an outwork for the projected Kaiser Wilhelm Canal. These "feelers" resulted in the celebrated Anglo-German Agreement of July 1, 1890. In this Germany gave up all claims to Uganda and Witu in the north, Nyasaland in the south, and some small districts in West Africa in return for a corridor from German Southwest Africa to the Zambesi (Caprivi's Finger), an extension of German East Africa westward to the great lakes and the Congo Free State, an extension of Kamerun to Lake Chad, and the cession of Heligoland; Zanzibar, Pemba and Nyasaland became British protectorates. Authorities have never agreed on the merits of this treaty, but as both Powers remained generally satisfied with the terms, it need not be seriously criticized.

Uganda remained for the time being outside the British fold. It was only after a military expedition under Captain Frederick Lugard had "pacified" the country that Mwanga, in 1892, placed his kingdom under the British East Africa Company's control. This was a temporary expedient, for the administration of the protectorate proved to be beyond the financial power of the Company, and only when the British Government reluctantly took the region from the Company's relaxing grasp in 1894 and 1895 was its future as a European colony fairly assured.

Here in East Africa as elsewhere the taste for colonial holdings proved to be expensive to gratify. Betwixt the signing of badly understood treaties with petty Negro chieftains and the development of thriving and loyal colonies lay a long road obstructed by native wars, official ignorance and corruption, lack of sufficient capital, ruthless exploitation, and social, race and labor problems. But both British and Germans persisted in attempts to work out efficient and economical administrations. By 1914 portions of East Africa were assuming a modern aspect. Uganda, separately administered, had a small but growing white population and extensive cotton and coffee lands tapped on the one hand by the Nile and on the other by the railway reaching the eastern shore of Lake Victoria. The British East Africa Protectorate, less favored by nature, was showing development along the line of the railway from Mombasa. The German protectorate displayed German industry in numerous spots and nowhere more than at Dar-es-Salaam, where an indifferent roadstead had become a fine modern port.

Thence a railway extended through sisal plantations to Lake Tanganyika and another approached Lake Nyasa.  But German East Africa by the fortunes of war became Tanganyika Territory and a British mandate, since when it has experienced the consequences of being less promising than numerous other wards of the greatest colonial Power.

In 1920 British East Africa became Kenya Colony and Protectorate and entered the second stage of growth characterized by a balancing colonial budget and a growing white population interested in self-government.  The political situation is made very difficult, however, first, by the determination of the Colonial Office to retain full control of the African natives, and second, by the presence of a large number of East Indians and Arabs, the former of whom, as British subjects, are determined to enjoy all rights accorded to English settlers.  The concession of limited representation in the Governor's Council, with a franchise discriminating strongly against non-European residents, has only aggravated the issue.  This promises to continue as one of the principal problems in future.

# CHAPTER III

## THE PROBLEMS AND CONSEQUENCES OF IMPERIALISM

### EXPANSION OF BRITISH SOUTH AFRICA

THE greater portion of Africa was staked out in a series of European national preserves within a decade after territorial competition in that continent became pronounced. The years intervening between the first group of partition agreements and the opening of the World War were marked by the consolidation of holdings and the settlement of conflicting claims, the penetration of lands which had escaped appropriation at the outset because of native power, isolation or lack of promise, and the growth of international jealousy as a characteristic feature of economic and political imperialism.

Among the several contests marking this period was the final struggle between Boer and Briton for control of the temperate portion of South Africa. This was a struggle without a parallel elsewhere in Africa since it arose less from the exigencies of European politics than from the vital needs of two dissimilar but vigorous colonizing peoples. In brief, the Boers were determined to maintain their institutions and independence at all costs. The British felt impelled to eradicate Negro slavery, to protect and support the missionary, to exploit all mineral wealth, and especially to maintain a free passage for trade and communication from the

Cape Colony to the lands beyond the Limpopo River and even beyond the Zambesi.

After a generation of intermittent *laissez faire* following the establishment and recognition of the Boer republics, new clashes began with the discovery of diamonds in the Kimberley region of the Orange Free State in 1871 and the opening up of rich gold fields on the Witwatersrand in the Transvaal in 1885. In each instance the rush for ready wealth drew to the mining fields a large and turbulent element, mainly British. The forcible annexation of the diamond fields by the Cape Colony as Griqualand West and the attempts of the Boers to control the Rand were potent causes of the bitter war which came at the end of the century.

Meanwhile, the failure of the Boers to reach the sea through Natal in 1837-1843, their exclusion from Basutoland in 1868, their loss of Griqualand West in 1871, the founding of British mission stations in Nyasaland and the Cape Colony's attempts at armed coercion, such as that which led to the Majuba Hill episode, placed the Boers in an extremely difficult position. Their only chance to escape complete envelopment appeared to lie in breaking over the paper barriers erected by the unsatisfactory London Convention of 1884 and in occupying such native lands as were still unclaimed. Some of the quick moves made with this in view might have succeeded but for the super-imperialist, Cecil Rhodes. Having already found enormous wealth in the diamond mines, he had consecrated himself and his fortune to the cause of British supremacy in South Africa. In 1888 he quietly obtained a treaty from the Matabele King, Lobengula, on the basis of which a

British South Africa Company was formed in 1889 and the protectorate of Rhodesia set up in 1890. This act completed the isolation of the Boer republics and left as their only alternatives complete submission to the will of Great Britain as exemplified in the Government of the Cape Colony or war to the extremity.

Organized Boer resistance probably would have broken down at this point but for the dominant personality and persistent hate of Paul Kruger, the very incarnation of the spirit of the trekkers, who served as President of the South African Republic from 1880 until the close of the Boer War. In his determination to expel the British from South Africa he had the active support of the Afrikander Bond, a patriotic Boer organization founded in the Cape Colony at the close of the brief campaign of 1881 to keep alive the spirit of unity and independence. It was Kruger's heavy taxation of the foreign element (Uitlanders) of the Rand and his refusal to grant any political concessions in return which provoked the next appeal to force in connection with the Jameson Raid of 1895.

This melodramatic expedition had its inception in the conviction of a considerable number of British imperialists that no concessions for the business interests in the Transvaal could be secured by peaceful means. Consequently a scheme was evolved, of which the principal authors were Cecil Rhodes, Prime Minister of the Cape Colony, and Dr. Leander Starr Jameson, administrator of Rhodesia under the British South Africa Company, for engineering a *coup d'état* in Johannesburg. Here, at a signal that armed assistance was coming, the Uitlanders were to revolt, seize arms and strategic positions, and hoist the British flag. At the crucial moment the conspiracy was mismanaged, and Dr. Jameson, who had invaded the Boer republic with a small mounted force, found himself isolated and surrounded by large Boer levies and was compelled to surrender at discretion.

The effects of this ill-starred venture were momentous. Rhodes was compelled to surrender his premiership, the Cape Government was discredited and even the British Colonial Office was suspected of complicity in the plot. Many of the Boers who had leaned toward coöperation with the British considered themselves betrayed and turned for guidance to Kruger, whose popularity had previously been waning before the counsels of more moderate leaders. But one of the most far-reaching consequences of all was the wave of sympathy for the Boer cause which swept over western Europe. Such evidences convinced Kruger and his aides that strong allies were at hand in case of a war for independence and were perhaps more instrumental than anything else in defeating all attempts at reasonable compromise made by moderates of both sides during the next four years.

The war which followed President Kruger's forty-eight hour ultimatum of October 9, 1899, to the Cape Government need not be detailed. It was characterized by initial over-confidence and faulty preparation on both sides and a preponderance of guerrilla fighting. As Kruger's European allies failed to materialize, the eventual outcome was scarcely in doubt. Yet the peace which was reached at Pretoria on May 31, 1902, had required an extensive pooling of the resources of the entire British Empire and the employment of more than a quarter of a million troops to subdue the Boer levies, which had never amounted to more than 40,000 men. In view of the sacrifices involved, the terms accorded to the Boers were generous. While the two Boer republics were irrevocably annexed, they were promised future responsible self-government, a recognition of their language, and a voice in the settlement of the native question. In 1906 and 1907, respectively, the Transvaal and the Orange Free State were accorded full political rights under the British Crown. Again the way was clear for a union of the South African states, a move which had failed deplorably on previous occasions, notably in 1876. Already the Customs Union, first formed in 1898, had been revived. The mutual desire to prevent another armed conflict, the rise of vexatious problems respecting tariffs and railways, and the imperative need of an early solution of the native question led by stages to a constitutional convention at Durban and Cape Town, and terms of union were agreed upon. These were legalized by the British Parliament in September, 1909.

Thus the Union of South Africa was created by the joint efforts of men who had lately been fighting one another on kop and veldt. The Union was not a federal structure but a strongly centralized state. The four former colonies, two Boer and two British, retained their identities as administrative districts, equal in status but not entirely uniform in political composition. The question of franchise was left open, since the Boer states were unwilling to accord to the blacks such rights as the latter enjoyed in the Cape Colony.

The political career of the new state was not destined to be as calm and successful as was augured. Almost from the outset the Boers dominated the Union Parliament and as the rival interests of agriculture and mining came to the fore irreconcilable Boer leaders advocated the secession of the Union from the British Empire. With the passing of Rhodes in 1902 and the lack of other English leaders of similar calibre, it was fortunate that the British cause found among the former Boer generals themselves such champions as Botha and Smuts, the former of whom was responsible for crushing the Boer revolt of 1914 and the latter for much of the coördination of the British Dominions during the latter part of the World War.

Difficult problems still call for solution. In a state where the whites are outnumbered by Negroes four to one, the native question is perennial. It is complicated in this instance by the presence of 140,000 disaffected Asiatics and by the insistent demands of East Indians that they be permitted to remove at will to South Africa. The South African protectorates and mandated Southwest Africa are sources of difficulty. But many of the older issues have been partially submerged in the rise of a Labor Party with its accompaniment of syndicalism. Also, the adoption of the principle of dominion equality with the mother country in the Imperial Conference of 1926 has tended to modify the Boer program of separation from the Empire and has assisted other influences in building up a common sentiment.

## THE SOUTH AFRICAN PROTECTORATES

The new period of European expansion ushered in by the Berlin Conference witnessed the establishment of a German protectorate in Southwest Africa and attempts of the Boers to erect the republics of Stellaland and Land of Goschen in Bechuanaland and the "New Republic" in Zululand. Aroused by these and similar aggressions in other parts of Africa, the British Government made some effort to prevent the seizure of other territories whose locations marked them as belonging within the imperial system. Basutoland and Bechuanaland therefore soon came directly under the control of British commissioners. In 1894 Swaziland, in the eastern Transvaal, received similar protection. These districts still remain as native reservations which it has been found unprofitable or impracticable to open up for white settlement and development.

Quite different has been the history of the region north of the Limpopo and south of the Central African lakes. Opened up first by Livingstone after 1849, it had long before his death become a favorite haunt of European hunters and traders from the Cape Colony and of Arab slavers from the East Coast. Following Rhodes' treaty of 1888 with Lobengula and the formation of the British South Africa Company came the beginning of white settlement in this vast area. In September, 1890, the town of Salisbury was laid out on the beautiful and salubrious plateau between the Limpopo and the Zambesi, a thousand miles from the nearest English settlement, and in succeeding months considerable numbers of farmers and speculators made their way into Rhodesia, founding new towns.

These Rhodesian settlements, however, had to undergo ordeal by fire before they were yet firmly established.  As in so many other similar instances, the native King, Lobengula, amazed at the white man's interpretation of his ill-considered promises, repented of his bargain and attempted to restore the *status quo ante* by complete extermination or expulsion of the whites.  The consequence was, naturally, that the higher civilization prevailed, much of Matabeleland was forfeited to the victors, and English settlement proceeded on a slower but firmer basis.  Other native troubles occurred subsequently, but after 1894 there was little doubt that Southern Rhodesia was destined to be primarily a white man's country.  Its political evolution has been characteristic of British frontier communities generally, beginning with control by a commissioner assisted by a small nominated council and reaching in 1922 the stage of full responsible government under a governor, a council and a legislative assembly.  The Company had meanwhile outlived its usefulness.  It had never paid a dividend, and in 1923 its control in Southern Rhodesia was terminated completely, leaving that colony essentially one of the minor British Dominions.

Here as in many other parts of Africa the presence of a preponderance of natives has given rise to difficult problems.  The creation of extensive native reserves, somewhat similar to the Indian reservations of North America, gave partial solution.  The presence of large numbers of able-bodied blacks has resulted in their being relied upon as the chief source of labor. Other leading problems touch the related matters of transportation and proposed incorporation in the South African Union. As to the latter, South Rhodesian sentiment definitely favors an independent national course.

Northern Rhodesia represents a much less promising situation. Not only does it lie nearer the Equator, but the table-lands north of the Zambesi are not so high as those to the south, hence they are less suitable for white colonization, being infested with the tsetse fly, the sleeping sickness and various fevers. Except along the course of the Zambesi, little was known of this vast region until after 1890, when small groups of pioneers began venturing into the wilderness. The Anglo-Portuguese treaty of 1891 conceded to Great Britain the territory lying between Angola and Mozambique, including the lands inhabited by the Barotse, which became known as Northwestern Rhodesia. In 1900 the entire region extending from the Zambesi to the borders of the Congo and German East Africa was made into two administrative districts, which were once again united as Northern Rhodesia in 1911. Since the termination of the British South Africa Company's control, this region has been controlled by a governor and council, but with a total white population of less than five thousand souls there has been little need for a legislative assembly. The isolation of this great territory has been considerably reduced by the extension from the South African Union of the railway which Cecil Rhodes dreamed would one day unite Cape Town with Cairo. The logic of position would link the future of Northern Rhodesia with Southern Rhodesia and Nyasaland, though whether a confederation of these territories will ever be achieved is problematical.

Nyasaland, the particular contribution of Livingstone to the British Empire, has been scarcely more attractive to European settlers than Northern Rhodesia. The promising work begun by English missionaries at Blantyre in the Shiré highlands about 1875 was quickly undone by Arab slave raids. The formation of the African Lakes Corporation in 1877 made possible the undoing of the Arabs and the opening up of the district lying south and west of Lake Nyasa. This, in turn, heralded the establishment of a British protectorate in 1891 and the further extension of the *pax Britannica*. The development of Nyasaland, however, has been slow, partly owing to the unsuitability of the climate for European life and partly to the lack of means of communication. The railway from Blantyre to Beira is one of the principal advantages of the fifteen hundred Europeans who are all but submerged in a native population a thousand times greater.

The attempts to develop self-sustaining, modern communities in Rhodesia and Nyasaland supply a variety of laboratory exercises in the problems of European expansion. No more instructive examples are needed to illustrate the process of European adaptation to different types of physical environment, the social and economic influences of primitive native groups and the usual inadequacy of private capital and enterprise alone to overcome the handicaps of a distant and isolated frontier. A more intensive study of

these South African colonies still in the earlier stages
of evolution would probably assist a better understanding of overseas colonization in other fields.

## THE CONTEST FOR THE SUDAN

The Sudan, because of its semi-arid nature and relative inaccessibility, long remained exempt from European influence and control. As the Nubia or Ethiopia
of ancient times, it ministered to Egypt through the
valley of the Nile, which forms the only natural road
to this extensive upland region. Egyptian control of
the Sudan began with the partial conquest of the independent Mohammedan chiefs of the plateau by Mehemet Ali in 1819. Khartum was the outpost of Egyptian authority at the accession of Ismail (1863), but
the next half dozen years saw its extension as far as
the sources of the Nile and from the kingdom of Darfur on the west to the Red Sea on the east.

For a considerable time this great area was ruled by
English governors appointed by the Khedive of Egypt
and considerable headway was made in establishing
order and suppressing an extensive traffic in slaves.
But the deposition of Ismail in 1879 ended this period
of progress and the Sudan became a prey to the greed
of Egyptian officials until the rise of Mohammed Ahmed, self-styled Mahdi, or Successor of the Prophet.

Starting on his remarkable career in 1881, the Mahdi
within two years had brought most of the Sudan completely under his control, annihilating the weak Anglo-
Egyptian forces sent against him. In 1884 at English
behest the Khedive determined to abandon the Sudan
completely, and secured the services of General Charles

George ("Chinese") Gordon for the difficult task of withdrawing the remaining Egyptian garrisons. Gordon found this a more serious task than had been anticipated, and, lacking effective Egyptian assistance, he appealed to the British Government for material aid. While the Liberal Cabinet procrastinated, Gordon and his handful of men were cut off in Khartum by the Mahdi's forces, and, before a relief expedition could reach them early in 1885, were exterminated. The entire Sudan thereupon relapsed into a species of anarchy which quickly wiped out all of the constructive work of the previous half century.

The restoration of European authority in the Sudan awaited changes in the personnel and policy of the British Government, the stimuli provided by the rapid appropriation of other parts of the continent by European rivals, and, more immediately, the loss of European prestige throughout North Africa as a consequence of the Italian disaster at Adowa (1896). A new penetration of the Sudan began in 1896, when General Kitchener undertook an advance from which there was to be no turning back. The Mahdist forces of the Khalifa, defeated in preliminary engagements, risked a decisive battle near Omdurman on September 2, 1898, in which nearly twenty thousand dervishes were destroyed. This victory, which, in its ultimate effects, ranks among the important battles of modern times, reëstablished Egyptian claims to the whole of the Sudan and paved the way for the reconstruction of the country.

The British were not yet free to exploit the Sudan as an Egyptian protectorate. Various nations chose to take the position that valid claims to the Sudan had ceased with its abandonment by Egypt in 1885. On this ground, the French had already taken exception to certain British engagements made during these years, notably the Anglo-Italian Protocols of 1891 and 1894 and the Belgian lease in 1894 of the Bahr-el-Ghazal region. In the hope of expanding French Central Africa to the eastern seaboard, the French denied the existence of any "effective occupation" as defined by the Berlin Act of 1885 and prepared to seize a point on the upper Nile, despite warning from England.

Immediately after the battle of Omdurman, General Kitchener was informed that a Major Marchand had raised the French flag at Fashoda, five hundred miles further up the Nile. With a despatch in keeping with the seriousness of the situation, Kitchener hastened with a mobile force to challenge the interloper. Marchand, confident of his position, refused to give way. An armed clash was averted only by the unwillingness of the two commanders to precipitate a major European war, and the question was referred to their respective governments.

News of the situation produced the greatest excitement in Europe and war spirit flared high in England and France. Doubtful of his Russian ally, and faced with the certain alternative of war, the French Minister, Delcassé, at length reluctantly withdrew his "envoy of civilization" from the Nile, and the conflict was averted. One of the most dangerous crises which arose at any time over the disposition of African territory was thus peaceably settled on March 21, 1899, with the signing of an Anglo-French Declaration compounding the differences in the Sudan. France surrendered her claims to Bahr-el-Ghazal and the ancient sultanate of Darfur, but retained the native kingdom of Wadai and some valuable oases together with the right of commercial access to the Nile. This settlement had already been preceded on January 19 by an Anglo-Egyptian Agreement, which provided for joint rule in the Sudan so ingeniously that the British were little encumbered in future in developing the region along their own lines.

The Sudan which was recovered in 1898 was vastly different from that lost in 1885. Three-fourths of the former population had perished; agriculture had almost ceased; nearly all live stock had disappeared. Under such circumstances, the outlook for the rehabilitation of the vast region was unpromising. Yet the sparsity of population proved to be a kind of blessing in disguise, since it left land in plenty for the growing of cotton on which the future prosperity of the Sudan depended. Only an adequate supply of water from the Nile was needed to make the country an exceedingly important economic area. The danger of injury to Egypt by overtaxing the Nile near its sources for irrigation purposes was met by the construction of enormous barrages both in Egypt and in the Sudan, of which the Senaar Dam is most noteworthy. These perform the double service of preventing the seasonal floods of former times and insuring an adequate supply of water for normal needs at all times.

The creation of the Egyptian Kingdom left the Sudan in British hands. This solved many of the problems of a joint administration, but new ones, born of Egyptian jealousy, quickly took their places. Egyptian acts of violence, such as the assassination of the Sirdar and Governor-General of the Sudan, Sir Lee Stack (1924), have frequently been traceable, at least in part, to the exclusion of Egyptians from the Sudanese administration.

Whatever grounds there may be for Egyptian complaints, it is certain that British success in developing the Sudan has been phenomenal. Railways penetrate every section; educational needs are being satisfied, notably through the remarkable work of Gordon College at Khartum; and a population once largely nomadic is now greatly enlarged and quite satisfied with sedentary and peaceful pursuits. The Sudan is perhaps the brightest jewel in the crown of European imperialism.

### THE RISE OF ITALIAN COLONIES: LIBYA

When Italy emerged a nation from the unification process, unduly conscious of her Roman heritage, she found herself without the dependencies and colonial trappings characteristic of a world power. To this sentimental need adhered more tangible motives for colonial acquisitions. Italy was largely overpopulated, poverty was widespread, trade was undeveloped. It was natural, therefore, that Italian imperialists should turn covetous eyes to the littoral of North Africa, which was anciently under Roman rule and more recently had become the home of thousands of Italians. Algeria, long since a French colony, was no land of promise to Italy, but Tunis, with its attractive lands, its many Italian merchants, and its proximity to Italy, appeared to be adapted in all respects to serve Italian needs.

Such plans as related to Tunis, however, were in vain. While Italy was yet consolidating her resources for an African venture, Great Britain proceeded to occupy Egypt, and France, in 1881, seized Tunis. Italian disappointment and pique were intense. Immediate designs on any other portion of North Africa were impracticable on many grounds. Crumbs of compensation, therefore, were sought on the eastern seaboard of the continent, where a slight hold had been obtained by an Italian steamship company immediately after the opening of the Suez Canal. The massacre of an Italian scientific party supplied an occasion for the seizure of the port of Massowah, the principal outlet of Abyssinia, and, profiting from the embarrassments of the British in the Sudan, the extensive colony of Eritrea was quickly staked out. In 1889, by the Treaty of Uccialli, King Menelek agreed to a certain supervision of his foreign relations by Italy, and Europe thereafter regarded Abyssinia as essentially an Italian protectorate.

A further step was taken toward securing the Abyssinian plateau, without which the arid coasts were of little use, when in 1890 Italy declared a protectorate over a thousand miles of the Somali coast south of Cape Guardafui. The presence of British and French spheres at the mouth of the Red Sea scarcely mattered to those who expected to emulate the French by obtaining control of the entire Abyssinian hinterland. But such plans were premature. In the battle of Adowa in 1896 the Italians suffered at the hands of the Abyssinians a terrible and decisive defeat. Dreams of a colony in Abyssinia vanished, and the Italian Government had as the net result of its first colonial ventures a heavy burden of expense and two vulnerable and valueless strips of seacoast.

The failure of designs on Abyssinia brought Italian aspirations back to the Mediterranean shores of Africa. Here the loss of Tunis to France had caused Italy in 1882 to form a Triple Alliance with the German Empire and Austria in order to maintain a balance of power, but this had not supplied the need for territory which might be colonized. East of Tunis lay the Turkish provinces of Tripoli and Cyrenaica, more distant and less desirable than Tunis, but as yet uncoveted by other Powers. The French Government already, with the generosity of a victor, had intimated its willingness that Italy create a sphere of special interest in Tripoli.

However, aside from the mere fact of Turkish suzerainty, there were several obstacles in the way of an Italian protectorate in Tripoli and Cyrenaica (Barca). In the Treaty of Paris in 1856 and again in the Treaty of Berlin in 1878 the integrity of Turkish dominions had been guaranteed by the Great Powers. This alone might have been no insuperable barrier, for such arrangements had been violated before by both Great Britain and France and neither Power was averse from a continuation of the process of Turkish dismemberment in Africa by Italy. But Austria and the German Empire, Italy's own allies, feared the repercussion that might be caused in Europe, and particularly in the Balkan States, by any further plundering of the Ottoman Empire and frowned, therefore, on Italian designs in that quarter.

In 1887 Great Britain formally agreed to support

Italian interests in Tripolitania, and although the Triple Alliance was renewed in that year, Italy soon displayed signs of lukewarmness toward her less considerate allies.[1] Presently Spain agreed to view with equanimity the African aims of Italy. But it was only in 1900 that France, in a secret agreement, definitely offered to abet Italian aspirations in Tripoli and Cyrenaica, with the reciprocal understanding that Morocco was to be regarded as a French sphere. The strengthening of the bonds between Turkey and Germany as a result of the Young Turk revolution of 1908 further weakened Italy's attachment to the Triple Alliance and gave rise to her resolution to act in the matter of Tripoli at the earliest practicable moment. The Racconigi Agreement with Russia in 1909, providing that "Italy and Russia engage themselves to regard with benevolence, the one Russia's interest in the question of the Straits, the other Italian interest in Tripoli and Cyrenaica," and the growing importance of Italy to both of the alliances, finally placed Italy in a most strategic position. Signor Giolitti, again assuming office as premier in 1911, determined upon immediate intervention in Tripolitania under guise of righting the wrongs suffered by Italian merchants and of abolishing slavery and other abuses, "infamies which could not be tolerated at the very gate of Europe."

On September 28, 1911, an ultimatum was despatched to the Porte reciting Italian grievances and demanding within twenty-four hours guarantees of reforms and protection of foreigners. The Turks, doubt-

[1] When the Triple Alliance was renewed in 1902 Germany and Austria reluctantly recognized Italy's ambitions and grudgingly accorded her a free hand.

ful of aid from any quarter, returned a conciliatory but futile reply, and the Turco-Italian War was begun. Two months later Italy annexed Tripoli and Cyrenaica by decree. But the war was not brought to conclusion with the anticipated ease. The ports in the African provinces were readily seized and Turkish resistance was reduced to a minimum, but the Tripolitans and desert Arabs stubbornly refused to submit. As the war reached a stalemate, the Italian people grew restless and diplomatic clouds darkened. To obtain a prompt and favorable decision, the Italian Government considered it necessary that they violate their categorical promises to localize the conflict and to make at least a demonstration against Constantinople. In the spring of 1912 several of the Turkish islands in the Ægean were occupied and two attempts were made to enter the Dardanelles, acts which openly violated existing international engagements respecting the Ottoman Empire. The members of both European alliances, foreseeing grave complications, sought ways in which to end the conflict without reviving the Eastern Question anew. The war was actually terminated by that most dreaded of dangers, an anti-Turkish rising in the Balkan States. To meet the new enemy, the Turks were driven to sign the Treaty of Lausanne on October 18, 1912, which tacitly surrendered the contested African provinces to Italy and left a generous legacy of troubles to Europe, including the immediate causes of the World War.

The treaty of Lausanne did not contain, even as a corollary, the acceptance of Italian rule in the new provinces. The entire hinterland was still to be conquered piecemeal. Scarcely had this process begun when the World War opened. The Turkish Sultan seized the opportunity to proclaim a Holy War in Tripolitania, and Italy, much preoccupied at the time, suffered serious reverses. At the close of the War, the subjugation of the interior was resumed, but only with indifferent success in some of the more remote sections.

A civil constitution issued in 1919 for the new provinces, sentimentally called Libya, extended Italian citizenship to the natives and provided for considerable degrees of self-government. More recently agricultural improvements and the introduction of sedentary occupations have greatly aided in the pacification of the colony. Inevitably the maintenance of large military forces together with serious mistakes in administration have saddled the Italian people with a heavy colonial burden, while the disinclination of the Italians to migrate to the colony has been a source of keen disappointment to the imperialists. Yet the lively interest of the Fascist régime in Libya has been reflected in progress along several lines, to which Italians with considerable reason point with pride.

## "INEVITABLE NECESSITY" IN MOROCCO

The Moroccan Empire was one of the last portions of Africa to come under European control. Protected from the winds of the Sahara by the Atlas Mountains, endowed with a wonderful climate and vast natural resources, but wholly lacking in political cohesion, it figured largely in late European diplomacy as a much coveted prize. The state itself in modern times was little better than a monument to the Arab conquests of the early Mohammedan era. Although nominally ruled by a descendant of the Prophet, actually chaos reigned and disorders abounded. The country owed its long immunity from European intervention less to its own inherent strength than to the mutual jealousies of the Powers themselves.

By the close of the nineteenth century, Morocco was surrounded on the landward side by territorial possessions of France. To complete the French imperial structure in Africa, this corner stone, itself slightly larger than France, was imperatively needed. The diplomatic barrage which was to precede actual attack began with the formation of the Triple Entente. In the Anglo-French Convention of 1899, by which the Fashoda incident was settled, it was recognized that "it appertains to France . . . whose dominions are coterminous for a great distance with those of Morocco, to preserve order in that country." Secret agreements, which contemplated Morocco as an eventual French protectorate, frequently punctuated the diplomatic relations of Great Britain, France, Italy and Spain in succeeding years.

These arrangements, largely the work of the French Foreign Minister, Delcassé, constituted notable victories, and France made haste to translate them into tangible accomplishments. In 1905 the moment seemed propitious. Brigandage was rife in numerous districts of the Shereefian Empire. The young Sultan, Abdul Aziz, had just obtained a large loan from Parisian bankers, and his predilections for European luxuries and high taxes had already seriously undermined his authority. Delcassé, therefore, confidently pressed upon the Sultan a French program of extensive reform, only to provoke a diplomatic crisis of the first magnitude.

The late negotiations of the western Powers concerning further appropriations of African territory, while carried on secretly, had inevitably come to the ears of the German Foreign Office. French short-sightedness in continuing completely to ignore German interests and susceptibilities while embarking on a program of intervention and reform in Morocco earned the reverses which followed. The German Kaiser himself, landing from his yacht at Tangier in March, 1905, and pledging German support to the Sultan as an independent sovereign, issued a direct challenge to the French Government. Abdul Aziz, grateful for the respite, proposed at German instigation that such Moroccan reforms as were necessary be considered by a general European conference. As France's ally, Russia, had lately been defeated and discredited at the hands of the Japanese, and as France herself was unprepared to accept the hazard of war, the protests of the conspiring Powers did not avail to counteract the German purpose of sharing in the Moroccan settlement. The over-zealous Delcassé resigned from the French Cabinet and a general conference was announced to meet at Algeciras in Spain early in 1906.

The Algeciras Conference had a most difficult task to perform. The Powers represented had to deal with the determination of Germany to humiliate France and to gain some real advantages for herself, perhaps by the partition of Morocco, and had to take into consideration the absolute refusal of France, in view of the insignificance of German economic interests in Morocco, to agree either to a partition of that country or to tolerate a large share of German control in shaping its destinies. Yet on the settlement of the controversy depended the peace of Europe. The factors which finally led to a pacific solution were, first, the partial recovery of Russia from the late war, second, the moderateness and sincerity of the French envoys, and, more than all, the pressure exercised by the United States for a reasonable compromise. President Roosevelt, in persuading Kaiser Wilhelm II to accept his scheme for a Franco-Spanish mandate in Morocco, did inestimable service to the cause of world peace as well as a distinct favor to France. This plan, embodied in the Algeciras Act of April 7, 1906, had the appearance of a German victory, since Morocco was recognized as independent under international supervision; but the placing of police powers in the hands of France and Spain gave recognition to their prime interests and enabled the former ere long to place a broad interpretation upon the settlement.

The continuation of disorders in Morocco, the growing prestige of the Triple Entente, and the rise of serious international problems in other quarters all contributed to the steady increase of French authority in Morocco after 1906, but they did not prevent the occurrence of two other crises before the manifest destiny of the country would be worked out. The dethroning of the dissipated Abdul Aziz during an anti-European uprising in 1907 and ill-judged action of German and French officials at Casablanca in 1908 caused a sudden flare of war spirit in both European states. The refusal of the French to be stampeded saved the day.

In December a new Sultan formally assumed all of the responsibilities of the previous régime and secured recognition, while a Franco-German Declaration, signed at Berlin in February, 1909, provided that no impediment be placed in the way of "the special political interests of France in Morocco," which was equivalent to the sanction of French pretensions.

For the second time the French Ministers assumed that no European obstacles remained to prevent their administration of the Moroccan Empire (outside of the Spanish zone of the Riff), reckoning without the express consent of the states other than Germany which had signed the Algeciras Act. This proved to be another costly blunder when, in 1911, the German Government objected to French methods of suppressing Moroccan disorders as violating the Berlin agreement. The stroke was shrewd, for other members of the Entente had not been parties to the negotiations of 1909 and hence had no ground for intervening in the renewed quarrel. But the German advantage was sacrificed when, on July 1, 1911, the entire Moroccan Question was suddenly reopened with the arrival of the German warship *Panther* at the port of Agadir "to protect the important German interests in the territory in question."

This move was correctly interpreted in France and Great Britain as signifying the German intent of securing a portion of Morocco before French control should be irrevocably established. The resulting tension kept the Great Powers on the verge of war for several months. The French, at once assured of complete support by their allies, displayed a willingness to consider making some concessions, but steadfastly refused, as before, to recognize any German position of special interest in Morocco or elsewhere. This firm position, the expressed intent of Great Britain to give unlimited support to France, the opening of the Italian attack on Tripoli, lack of popular support at home, together with a severe financial panic all influenced German imperialists to recede from their extreme demands. French and German representatives thus were enabled to reach an agreement embodied in the Moroccan and Congo Conventions, signed on November 4, 1911. In substance, the first of these gave France a free hand in Morocco on condition that German interests be protected, while the second transferred to the German Empire over 100,000 square miles of French Congo, giving an outlet to the Congo basin at two points for the hinterland of German Kamerun.

The settlement of November 4, presently adhered to by all the signatories of the Algeciras Act, was received by a large group of imperialists in Germany as less than half a loaf and in France with bitterness because of the partial spoliation of French Equatorial Africa. There was, however, no longer any considerable doubt as to the position of France in Morocco, and a program of quiet military occupation of the country was undertaken at once, pending the establishment of a formal protectorate late in 1912.

The new régime set up in French Morocco was typical of African protectorates. The Sultan continued as nominal ruler, through whom or in whose name all government is carried on. The real source of authority, under the French Foreign Office, is the French Resi-

dent-General, who must approve all governmental de-
crees, and to whom is entrusted the considerable task of
preserving internal order, on the one hand, and of supervising foreign relations, on the other. Local governmental machinery has been left unchanged as far as
possible, though for supervisory purposes the country
has been made into military districts and subdivided
into posts, circles, and stations.

At the time of the establishment of the protectorate,
the French were in control of but a small portion of the
country. The occupied area has been steadily enlarged
until only a few remote sections remain to be incorporated into the system. Much of French success
in the administration of Morocco has been due to the
remarkable character of the first Resident-General,
Marshal Lyautey. His appointment to this responsible
post was earned by the facility with which he established order after the creation of the protectorate; but
it has been amply justified by his reliance on fairness
and diplomacy rather than military authority. His interest in the welfare of the governed has made the protectorate a source of real strength to the French nation.

In the pacification and development of Morocco, improved communication has played an important part.
Railway construction has been so designed as to facili-
tate troop movements and simultaneously to open up
the rich phosphate and iron regions and those capable
of agricultural development as well. The extensive
employment of French capital in development projects,
the cancellation of German interests by the tariff dis-
crimination all have redounded largely to French advantage, and Morocco gives promise, although remain-

ing a protectorate, of becoming a principal bulwark of the French colonial system.

The Spanish, controlling about one-twelfth of Morocco, have been vastly less successful than the French. Faulty methods of dealing with native chiefs have prevented any extensive pacification in this zone and have made Spanish Morocco an expensive burden to the Spanish nation. At times, real control has extended no further than the immediate vicinity of the coast towns. A well directed campaign launched by the wild tribes of the Riff in 1923 caused the Spanish heavy losses and presently involved the French as well. Three years of hard fighting were necessary to bring about the surrender of the famous bandit-chieftain, Abd-el-Krim. Nevertheless, the Spanish have become strongly imbued with the idea that colonies are necessary adjuncts of a Great Power. Consequently, they have doggedly held on to their Moroccan zone, which can scarcely ever become a source of revenue or strength, and have even cherished hopes of acquiring the Tangier zone, internationalized by the Franco-Spanish Protocol of November 27, 1912.

### AFRICA AND THE WORLD WAR

By the end of the year 1912 the African continent had been almost completely appropriated. All of the Powers with definite colonial aspirations had participated in the spoiling contest which, as lands of value grew scarce, had become increasingly strenuous. The map of Africa disclosed the inevitable result: the stronger nations held the most extensive and promising territories, leaving the less desirable lands for the weaker. Probably in no single instance was European territorial greed or ambition satisfied. Cherished colonial plans had often fallen short of realization. The tardy hope of the Portuguese that they might secure a solid strip across the continent uniting Angola and Mozambique was foredoomed to failure. Similar plans of the Germans for connecting their West Coast acquisitions with German East Africa were infringed upon by the anomalous Belgian Congo and frustrated by the British and French. France, by dint of remarkable industry, had succeeded in creating an enormous empire, but it failed to reach the Nile and the Red Sea and its symmetry was marred by numerous enclaves, particularly by Kamerun after 1911. The Italians were only partially consoled by the acquisition of Libya for their earlier failures in Abyssinia, which left their Somali holdings worthless. Even the British, entering the contest with the most favorable handicaps, could not contemplate the map without bitter reflections. They had allowed many of the choicest portions of the continent to fall into the hands of their rivals, and had failed to preserve an "all red" corridor for the realization of the Cape-to-Cairo railway plan.

It seems remarkable at first, in view of the importance attached to colonial possessions and the many serious crises which had developed in the course of their acquisition, that the whole of Africa was parceled out without having provoked a war among the participants. On a number of occasions since the continent had been marked for European exploitation the clashing interests of super-imperialistic states had produced situations of the gravest character. But in one way or

another peaceful solutions to these had always been
found, and the more optimistic observers were inclined
to see in their outcome only so many indications of the
increasing likelihood of world peace. A closer exami-
nation of these crises would appear to show that generally war was averted not so much because of any
fundamental antipathy to an appeal to arms but rather
because of a conviction on the part of one or more of
the contestants that a resort to force at the time would
be impracticable, unprofitable, or unnecessary. Certainly each threat of war left its legacy of bitterness
and suspicion, and, while some difficulties were neu-
tralized by subsequent understandings and political
coalitions, their increasing frequency as the twentieth
century opened forecast a time when compromise might
no longer be effectual.

It is more than passing ironical, nevertheless, that
the last moves in the appropriation of Africa, the
French acquisition of Morocco and the Italian conquest
of Tripoli, had apparently been carried to successful
issue when the delicate balance of interests in the Balkans was upset by Ottoman reverses in North Africa
and the World War eventuated. In this great struggle,
which owed so many of its underlying causes to African
quarrels, numerous agreements on which the partition
of Africa had been based were automatically reduced
to "scraps of paper." A new dispensation awaited the
diplomacy of war.

African questions, along with others, were fought out
principally on the Western Front after 1914, but the
material and psychological importance of African territories and their probable value as pawns in peace ne-

gotiations made Africa also an important theatre of war. In this field the Germans, although at a disadvantage, gave good accounts of themselves. Not only did they defend their own colonies with great fortitude and persistence, but they scored elsewhere. Through their alliance with Turkey, they attempted to bring about a general uprising of the millions of African Moslems against the Entente Powers. Except for risings of no serious consequence in Libya and the eastern Sudan, their efforts miscarried. German plans were more nearly successful in aiming Turkish attacks at the Suez Canal. More serious still was the German-inspired South African rebellion, which narrowly missed resulting in a British catastrophe.

However, it was a foregone conclusion that the German colonies would eventually be taken during an extended war in which the Entente allies retained control of the seas. German Southwest Africa was conquered with some difficulty in 1915 by white troops from the South African Union. Togoland and Kamerun were captured by converging British and French columns, with some Belgian assistance, in campaigns lasting a year and a half. In East Africa the British carried the day with some reinforcement from the Belgians and Portuguese. German resistance was largely ended by 1916, though in a few places hostilities continued until the close of the War in Europe.

As a result of the War, the German flag disappeared from Africa. At another time in European history the German colonies would have been annexed forthwith. Those members of the Entente having African interests were given shares of the German territories at the Versailles Peace Conference, to be sure, but only as mandates under the League of Nations. Thus, Togoland and Kamerun were divided into British and French mandate zones, with the exception of that portion of Kamerun alienated to Germany in 1911, which was reannexed to the French Congo. German East Africa became a British mandate as Tanganyika Territory, excepting the two populous provinces of Ruanda-Urundi, which became adjuncts of the Belgian Congo. All these were to be administered as "B" mandates, that is, the mandatories are bound to "respect the rights and safeguard the native population" and to maintain the "open door." But German Southwest Africa was awarded to the South African Union, its conqueror, as a "C" mandate, which permitted its incorporation into the administrative system of the Union—a scarcely veiled form of annexation. In this way the number of African Powers was reduced by one, and the map of Africa was to that extent simplified. But blocks of solid color on the map do not necessarily spell better conditions or more rapid progress in such areas.

## THE EFFECTS OF EUROPEAN IMPERIALISM

It is still too soon since the hasty appropriation of Africa to assess many of the results with a great measure of confidence. The partition and exploitation of the continent has not been too recent, however, to have been very instructive in numerous ways, for the record of imperialism has been indelibly written.

One consequence has been the intensification, often to an unhealthy degree, of the strong national sentiment characteristic of more aggressive states. Likewise, democratic tendencies have been checked in some measure by the consciousness of power over dependent peoples. But such effects of imperialism have been, on the whole, less deplorable than the extremely heavy financial burdens inevitably connected with a program of territorial expansion overseas. To the vast outlay required for surveys, pacification of natives, establishing and subsidizing colonial administrations, and carrying out development programs have almost invariably been added other large expenditures for secret diplomacy and for armaments in the interests of colonial defense. The diversion of wealth for these purposes has not infrequently stood in the way of badly needed improvements at home. Then if the World War be ascribed in large measure to the animosities growing out of international competition in Africa, it will be clearly evident that the returns from African holdings must indeed be immense ever fully to justify the cost.

Considerable economic advantages have already been derived from Africa. For years most of the world's supply of diamonds and an appreciable part of the world's gold was produced in South Africa. Until the recent development of new rubber producing regions, Equatorial Africa was almost the sole source of this valuable commodity. The Sudan has become almost synonymous with cotton, though other parts of Africa annually increase their production of plant fibres. These are but conspicuous examples of a long and varied list of African products on which the industrial world has come to rely. The ultimate potentialities of the continent have scarcely yet been estimated.

Since European imperialism and the present type of

European civilization rest on an industrial basis, the capacity of Africa to absorb European manufactured goods is nearly as important as its production of raw materials. Over most of the continent this capacity has been growing at a very fair rate and in proportion to the cultural development of the inhabitants. A greater rate of flow of European colonists with their ready developed needs to some of the more salubrious districts would be economically desirable, but Europeans have shown no great disposition to migrate to Africa except in the south, where the colonizing process began long before the exploitation of the whole continent had been dreamed of.

Along other than economic lines European imperialism has not been without reward. Africa has served as a vast experimental station to the advantage of the colonial Powers in particular and the world in general. It has afforded unique opportunities for the training of officials for public service. Experiments in colonial administration have shed much light on problems in political theory. Both natural and applied sciences have profited from the study of African flora and fauna, geological structure and minerals, and natural phenomena, as the social sciences have been enriched by the knowledge of previously unknown stages of human culture. The benefits of European control to the peoples of Africa are problematical. It was not philanthropy which took the white man to Africa, and he has not remained primarily for philanthropic reasons. He has, in one way or another, expected to derive material profits from his enterprise. In order to do so, he has resorted to all kinds of forced labor, oppressive taxes and levies, and cruel punishments. He has even drafted the native to fight his wars. He has frequently expropriated the best lands of the native that he might enjoy them himself. On the whole, his concern for the welfare of the native has been incidental.

Moreover, the assumption has not been borne out that European manners and morals necessarily improve on native ways. Too generally European food and clothing, alcoholic liquors and diseases have proved deleterious and destructive to the health and vitality of the native. Even mission stations have often been unconscious agents of evils as serious as those they have sought to remedy. Elsewhere European vices have generally been more acceptable to the native than European virtues, and it has been disclosed in a disconcerting variety of ways how thin a veneer is our boasted western civilization when brought into contact with lower types of culture under unfavorable climatic and other environmental conditions.

On the other hand, keeping in mind the fact that conditions have varied widely according to the racial character of the native, methods and abilities of European nations, and natural environment, it may be pointed out that certain benefits have accrued to native peoples over wide areas. Incessant and savage tribal wars have been ended and cruel and barbarous rites and practices abolished. The myriad diseases of Africa are being checked or their effects mitigated. The slave trade has virtually vanished. Life and property have become relatively secure, as they never were prior to the establishment of European dominion. The extension of means of communication and the introduction of new articles of food provide insurance against famine. And in general the knowledge of the native has been increased and his efficiency in any scheme of life considerably raised. European withdrawal from Africa at the present stage or within a long period of years to come would leave only anarchy and chaos.

Two factors, in particular, have coöperated in relegating to the past the worse features of European rule. The first in point of time is the growth of a civilized conscience, often described as one of the by-products of the Industrial Revolution. This first expressed itself through missionary and humanitarian societies, later through the regulative acts of national governments, and more recently through the work of the League of Nations. It is a far cry from a "white man's burden" resting on the conviction that "the lower civilizations must give way before the advance of the higher" to the acceptance, as the basis of the mandate system, of the pronouncement that "in questions of [colonial] sovereignty the interests of the populations concerned must have equal weight with the equitable claims of the government whose title is to be determined." The Berlin Act of 1885 recognized the principle of European trusteeship in Africa. The Permanent Mandates Commission of the League of Nations, with more effect than had been contemplated by its sponsors, has carried the idea still further. Most of the African Powers have been constrained to carry into the administrations of their colonies extensive and expensive improvements not based on the expectation of proportionate increase in revenues.

The second and perhaps more important factor is

the growing realization that since much of Africa is permanently unsuited for white colonization, its future depends to a considerable extent on the treatment of the native. This forward view undoubtedly has entered considerably into the calculations of the several colonial offices in making appropriations for health surveys, educational programs, and improved systems of justice. While there is a genuine and growing interest in the native *per se*, he is still regarded more as one of the natural resources of the country, perhaps, than as a deserving ward.

Other forces are also operating to change the relative status of European and native in Africa. The very reaction of European methods on the native, whether wild Taureg or lowly Hottentot, tends to make him more capable of maintaining and improving his position. Education is not necessarily formal, and African peoples have been learning apace the secrets of European superiority. Formal education will but accelerate the lessening of the gulf between the white man and the man of color. The World War, in which the African native and the European often fought side by side, considerably disillusioned the former by giving him bases of comparison, hence its tendency has been to equalize the relations of the two. These developments will not necessarily make for future peace between the peoples of Europe and those of Africa, but in time they will certainly affect the character of European control.

# BIBLIOGRAPHICAL NOTE

A subject as comprehensive as *European Imperialism in Africa* naturally has given rise to a fairly extensive, though ill-balanced, literature. The books in this field comprise a considerable variety of works, voluminous for some regions and periods, distressingly meagre for others. The titles selected for inclusion in the list below have been chosen with the object of supplying a general and representative reading list. Although preference has generally been given to recent writings, some of the older accounts, especially those prepared by participants in the African adventure, can on no account be omitted.

No single work covers in satisfactory detail the whole of our subject. One of the earliest and most authoritative treatises on European enterprise in Africa, *The Partition of Africa*, by J. S. Keltie (2d ed., 1895), is still perhaps the most valuable general survey down to the last decade of the nineteenth century. Sir H. H. Johnston's brief *History of the Colonization of Africa by Alien Races* (1899) covers a wide scope with emphasis on early European activity in Africa, while Sir Charles Lucas' equally brief and comprehensive study, *The Partition and Colonization of Africa* (1922), is more concerned with the recent period. For the nineteenth century, an excellent account, though decidedly French in flavor, is Jean Darcy's *Cent Années de Rivalité Coloniale* (1907). H. A. Gibbons in *The New Map of Africa* (1918), sketches European interests to the close of the World War in a chatty yet stimulating way, and N. D. Harris, in his textbook on *Europe and Africa* (1927), brings his subject into the post-war period in uninspiring detail.

## I

Convenient sources for European enterprise in Africa during the Old Colonial Era are relatively few. Sir H. H.

Johnston's *The Opening Up of Africa* (1911), in the Home University Library, is the most useful short survey of this period. The two volumes of W. C. Abbott's *The Expansion of Europe* (1918) teem with items of interesting and pertinent information with emphasis on the European background. European beginnings in Africa are treated at some length in G. M. Theal's *The Portuguese in South Africa* (1896); A. Marvaud's *Le Portugal et Ses Colonies* (1912); J. P. Oliveira Martins' *The Golden Age of Prince Henry the Navigator* (trans., 1914), and more briefly in *The Oxford Survey of the British Empire: Africa* (Vol. III, 1914). The standard source of general information on Africa at the time of the partition is Keith Johnston's *Africa* (3d ed., 1884), which contains fairly reliable statistics of all kinds and a number of particularly fine maps.

Full and interesting accounts of early British activity in South Africa are found in G. M. Theal's *The History of South Africa since 1795*, vol. I (1908); A. W. Tilby's *English People Overseas*, vol. V: *South Africa* (1912); and Sir C. P. Lucas' *Historical Geography of the British Colonies*, vol. IV, pt. I (1913), and accounts of varying length occur in most of the histories of the British Empire.

The French Algerian Expedition is treated in detail in G. Esquer's *La Prise d'Alger, 1830* (1923). Other phases of French expansion in North Africa are well discussed in Alfred Rambaud's *La France Coloniale* (7th ed., 1895); Paul Leroy-Beaulieu's *L'Algérie et la Tunisie* (2d ed., 1897), and Henri Lorin's *L'Afrique du Nord; Tunisie-Algérie-Maroc* (1908).

Numerous writers have discussed the development of European interests in Egypt. The causes of European rivalry here in the eighteenth and nineteenth centuries are newly defined in H. L. Hoskins' *British Routes to India* (1928). George Young's *Egypt* (1927) gives a general but somewhat superficial account of Egypt during the last two centuries. The events leading from the temporary European occupation in 1798 and the years following to the assumption of complete responsibility in Egypt by the British are pictured in A. E. P. B. Weigall's semi-biographical *History of Events in Egypt, 1798-1914* (1915), and are more seriously and authoritatively treated in Lord Cromer's *Modern Egypt* (2 vols., 1908) and in the *Cambridge Modern History*, vol. XII (1910). The British occupation itself is well delineated in Sidney Low's *Egypt in Transition* (1914), Sir Alfred Milner's *England in Egypt* (1892; 13th ed., 1920), and W. S. Blunt's *Secret History of the British Occupation of Egypt* (1922).

## II

Suggestions for reading on the opening up of Africa should not fail to include accounts written by some of the great explorers of "Darkest Africa." Of these, David Livingstone's *Missionary Travels and Researches in South Africa* (1857; other eds. 1872 and 1912) and Henry M. Stanley's thrilling *Through the Dark Continent* (2 vols., 1878) have long been household classics. Sir Samuel W. Baker, *The Nile Tributaries of Abyssinia* (1867, 6th ed., 1882), Paul B. Du Chaillu, *Explorations and Adventures in Equatorial Africa* (1861), George Schweinfurth, *The Heart of Africa* (2 vols., 1873), and A. H. S. Landor, *Across Widest Africa* (1907), are all graphic accounts of pioneer explorers in various parts of the African wilderness. R. Coupland's *Kirk on the Zambesi* (1928), based on Kirk's diary and government archives, contributes notably to our knowledge of the unveiling of South East Africa.

The rapid staking out of national claims in Africa produced a tortuous diplomacy, much of which has not yet been recounted. A key to the events of the eighties and nineties is supplied by A. B. Keith's *The Belgian Congo and the Berlin Act* (1919), more readable and more accurate than the basic monograph of J. S. Reeves, *The International Beginnings of the Congo Free State* (1894). H. M. Stanley's *The Congo and the Foundings of Its Free State* (2 vols., 1885) is an interesting but colored account by one of the founders. Keltie in his *Partition of Africa*, previously mentioned, and J. H. Rose in *The Development of the European Nations, 1870-1921* (6th ed., 1922), vol. II, offer excellent accounts of the partitioning process.

British interests in West Africa are outlined in A. B. Keith's *West Africa*, vol. III of Lucas' *Historical Geography of the British Colonies* (2d ed., 1913). Those of the French are best set forth in Félicien Challaye's *Le Congo Française: La Question Internationale du Congo* (1909) and W. M. Sloane's *Greater France in Africa* (1924). The situation in Nyasaland and Uganda is the theme of Captain F. D. Lugard, author and militant hero of *The Rise of Our East African Empire* (2 vols., 1893), whose *The Dual Mandate in British Tropical Africa* (1922) authoritatively treats of the clash of interests in East Africa after 1880. *East Africa: A New Dominion* (1927), by Maj. A. G. Church, is concerned with British success in developing this tropical colony. These books on East Africa are well supplemented by A. F. Calvert's *German East Africa* (1927). Overlapping claims and interests in the heart of Africa find expression in A. W. Tilby's *English People Overseas*, vol. IV: *Britain in the Tropics* (1912); J. K. Vietor's *Geschichtliche und Kulturelle Entwickelung Unserer Schutzgebiete* (1913) and Evans Lewin's *The Germans and Africa* (1915). Mary E. Townsend's dispassionate *Origins of Modern German Colonialism, 1871-1885* (1921) supplies a useful background for a study of Anglo-German colonial rivalry.

### III

British interests and accomplishments in South Africa have frequently been described. Volume V of Tilby's *English People Overseas*, devoted to *South Africa* (1912), gives a satisfactory and readable account of a century of effort in this field. The entire period from the Portuguese explorations to the Boer War is covered by G. M. Theal, the leading authority on South African history, in his *South Africa* (1900), one of the Story of the Nations Series. The salient points in the contest between Briton and Boer are well delineated in James Bryce's inimitable *Impressions of South Africa* (1897), J. A. Hobson's *The War in South Africa, 1892-1902* (1906), and in the fairly recent biographical studies of *Cecil Rhodes* (1921), by Basil Williams; *The Life of Jameson* (2 vols., 1922), by Ian Colvin; and *General Botha* (1924), by S. C. B. (Earl) Buxton. More recent developments are traced in E. A. Walker's *A History of South Africa* (1927). *The Colonial Office List* is a standard source of extremely useful information on all phases of recent British colonial developments.

In addition to the chapters on the Anglo-Egyptian Sudan included in most of the recent books on Egypt, the problems of the Sudan have been discussed more particularly in G. Dujarric's *L'État Mahdiste du Soudan* (1901), Yacoub Artin Pasha's *England in the Sudan* (1911), a descriptive work, and P. F. Martin's *The Sudan in Evolution* (1921).

The later stages of the appropriation of the African continent, which had such an important bearing on the opening of the World War, are treated in most of the histories of recent European diplomacy. Particular mention should be made of G. P. Gooch's brilliant and substantial *History of Modern Europe, 1878-1919* (1923). Special aspects of African problems are dealt with in E. D. Morel's *Morocco in Diplomacy* (1912), Charles Lapworth's pro-Italian *Tripoli and Young Italy* (1912), and T. Tittoni's self-justifying *Italy's Foreign and Colonial Policy* (trans., 1914).

A good, short summary of the campaigns in Africa during the World War is supplied by H. C. O'Neil's *The War in Africa and in the Far East* (1915). A longer account, no less readable, is Sir Charles Lucas' *The Empire at War*, vol. IV (1925). Probably the most thorough study of European policies and methods in Africa before the War and of problems arising since is G. L. Beer's *African Questions at the Paris Peace Conference* (1923). *The Native Problem in Africa* (2 vols., 1928), by R. L. Buell, is an able and comprehensive piece of work, interest in which would be enhanced by a reading of E. D. Morel's *The Black Man's Bur-*

*den* (1920), T. J. Jones' *Education in Africa* (1922) and N. Ley's *Kenya* (1924).

The basic factors involved in European enterprise in Africa have been somewhat difficult of evaluation. They are treated historically in P. T. Moon's *Imperialism and World Politics* (1924), and more philosophically in J. A. Hobson's *Imperialism: A Study* (1902). Imperialism is also briefly discussed in the third chapter of F. C. Dietz's *The Industrial Revolution* (1927), one of the Berkshire Studies in European History.

# INDEX